Five Easy Pieces

A Memoir

Craig Thomas Blake

Wingspan Press

Published in the United States and the United Kingdom
by WingSpan Press, Livermore, CA
The WingSpan name, logo and colophon are the trademarks of WingSpan Publishing.

Publisher's Cataloging-in-Publication data
Names: Blake, Craig Thomas, author.
Title: Five easy pieces : a memoir / Craig Thomas Blake.
Description: Includes bibliographical references and index. | Livermore, CA: Wingspan Press, 2022.
Identifiers: LCCN: 2021923583 | ISBN: 978-1-63683-501-3 (hardcover) | 978-1-63683-022-3 (paperback) | 978-1-63683-980-6 (ebook)
Subjects: LCSH Blake, Craig Thomas. | San Francisco (Calif.)--Biography. | San Francisco (Calif.)--20th century--History. | University of California, Berkeley--Biography. | BISAC BIOGRAPHY & AUTOBIOGRAPHY / Personal Memoirs
Classification: LCC F869.S39 .B53 2022 | DDC 979.4/61/092--dc23

First edition 2022

Printed in the United States of America

www.wingspanpress.com

1 2 3 4 5 6 7 8 9 10

Author's Note

The stories in this book reflect the author's recollection of events. Some names, locations, and identifying characteristics have been changed to protect the privacy of those depicted. Where there is dialogue, it has been recreated from the author's memory.

In Memory of My Parents,

Reinhart & Grace Blake

Table of Contents

Acknowledgements

The inspiration for this set of memoirs is largely owed to the works of Stephen King, particularly his own memoir, *On Writing,* which played a role in the way I went about writing what you are about to read.

Also helpful was, *The Memoir Workbook: A Step-by-Step Guide to Help You Brainstorm, Organize, and Write Your Unique Story*, by C.S.Lakin.

Most importantly, I wish to recognize all the individuals, well over one hundred at last count, who are a part of my story.* Although a very few aren't cast in a positive way (and for those I have used pseudonyms), most of my "characters" had a very positive impact on my life.

I thank them, one and all.

Craig Thomas Blake

* Exhibit VII-a through Exhibit VII-f provides a list of characters

"In all our searching,
the only thing we've found
that makes the emptiness bearable
is each other."

Carl Sagan

Prologue

Prologues start at the beginning, right? Maybe, sometimes. I'm actually writing this particular prologue after completion of the work, however. Otherwise, I wouldn't be able to address what's to follow, would I?

What is this writing all about? Is it a memoir which is typically defined as using one's life experiences in service of a larger theme?

Or is it an autobiography which is simply a story of one's life?

While it's a little bit of each, I prefer to think of it more in terms of the former, but in five parts, or "five pieces," each one designed to underscore a particular aspect of my life and how that aspect related to the larger picture. And with each of those five pieces subdivided into several episodes.

The first piece sets the stage for the pieces that follow. It tells of my early years and some of the things that happened with my family.

The second involves my learning experiences during the college years.

The third discusses my post-college life, the work I did, and the people I worked with.

The fourth is largely about some of the pastimes I am pursuing in retirement.

The last piece is both retrospective as well as forward looking, culminating in some ideas about enriching one's life.

Although the five pieces are organized chronologically starting with my early years and proceeding to the present day, the individual episodes themselves, while numbered, are arranged more in terms of topics than chronology.

Throughout the body of this work I have attempted to look at my life in terms of the times in which I lived. So, as you read on, be prepared for a bit of history in the bargain.

Every memoir has an audience, whether intended or not. Who is my intended audience for this memoir? Who do I really want to read it? That would be my two sons; I hope they both read it. Some of it they will like and perhaps even benefit from, while there may be other parts they knew little or nothing about and find concerning. After all, one of my goals in writing is to be as open, honest and candid as possible. There's no "sugar coating" here, that's for sure.

Perhaps my two daughters-in-law will read it and maybe they too will take away something from that reading.

And, lastly, maybe my five grandchildren will one day take a look at the stories herein and in so doing learn something interesting about me as well as my generation, the baby boom generation.

That doesn't mean that others should not read it or that they couldn't learn anything from it. Because I think there are all kinds of lessons contained herein, lessons that I would like to share with others.

Maybe my spouse of over two decades would appreciate knowing more about the years that followed that period and what I believe I have accomplished over those years.

Perhaps my partner would enjoy learning more about my experiences before we first met.

I imagine that some of the friends and relatives I mentioned in my story would also enjoy perusing it.

And I say to those beyond my "social-circle" of friends and relatives who may stumble on this memoir in "five easy pieces," my underlying intent (at the risk of sounding a bit "preachy") is that whoever you are, you should somehow, someway benefit from it.

Why did I start this in the first place? Well, I was inspired by a friend from long ago who I only recently reconnected with. He told me that he spent much of his time writing about various life experiences. And I thought, if I were to do likewise, there's no better time than the present. I am 74 years old, after all.

With respect to that age, I recently used what is called a "John Hancock Life Expectancy Calculator" to get a handle on how long I might live, given my current age. I'll discuss the results more thoroughly in future episodes.

Although I liked the Hancock results, I found them to be highly improbable. Depending upon what assumptions are made, particularly those relating to blood pressure and the frequency of exercising (of which I do little at present), I calculated at the low end an expectation of reaching 89 years of age. With more generous assumptions, the figure jumps to 101. I, frankly, couldn't believe that. It's terribly optimistic. I mean, how many folks do you know who live more than 100 years?

So, what if I'm right that it's overly optimistic and I have only a few more years to live? What would I do with those few years?

Well, I was hoping to find the answer to that as I went through the process of writing. I said at the outset that I'm writing this prologue after I have finished the body of the memoir. But I may have to go back through it all over again to find the answer to that question. And I won't be totally satisfied if it isn't there.

Oh, and a couple more things. First, there are bound to be some aspects of my life and/or the times in which I lived, that I haven't quite gotten right as I stretch my memory to its limits. Things like dates or people or places. Maybe someone reading this will point out something that I didn't get right. That's okay. That will increase the value of my effort. And it would give me an excuse to write another (and perhaps, more accurate) memoir.

The second point relates to the way I've handled the various experiences I've had throughout the years. I've tried my best not to be redundant about those experiences; however, in some cases I refer to the same matter in more than one episode. There is usually a good reason for that, and most of the time that reason involves a different context or setting.

As a final point, I realize that I've mentioned my current age more than once throughout the story. Again, it usually has to do with the context of that particular episode.

I think that I've covered all I need to cover in this Prologue.

I appreciate your taking the time to read what follows. And I'm hoping that you will enjoy reading it as much as I did writing it.

First Piece: In the Beginning

1 - Some Background

To borrow from the opening of the 1970 film, *Love Story,* "where do I begin?"

How about: My name is Craig Thomas Blake, and I'm an alcoholic?

Maybe not. That's definitely a little harsh, but be patient, as I do need to address that subject a little later.

Instead, let's try this: I was born on the second of November (a Scorpio, no less), in 1946, and a baby boom baby at that. A whole generation, referred to as "baby boomers," came about that first year and continued through 1964 (interestingly the year I graduated from high school). I was on the cusp, being born just shortly after the official end of World War II.

The notion of a baby boom resulted when those married men serving in the military came home from the War and began to restart their families. Unfortunately, not all those who served came home.

My father never had to confront that reality, however, avoiding service with the military during the War. Ironically, I would do the same, avoiding service during the Viet Nam War many years later.

While I managed to "dodge" conscription into that War, I don't think of my father in that context since he was included in a grouping of "reserved occupations" during World War II. Roughly five million men fell into those occupations which were considered essential at the time. Interestingly, his occupation as a grocery store manager was one of them, I was told by my parents.

Thirty years later I would avoid military service for quite a different reason, but I'll provide an explanation of that later on.

Obviously, I don't recall much of anything about the year 1946. Memories can't go back that far. Sigmund Freud called it "infant amnesia." My first recollection of life itself? That would be around the age of four or five years. Just before I left for the infamous first trip to kindergarten. But there's not all that much to say about that experience. It was probably the same experience that every child that age has. I do recall one thing, however. I was scared out of my wits so mom said she would be waiting outside the door the whole time I was inside. She did say that. And I saw her there until I got engrossed in kindergarten type of stuff.

But she lied.

Once she could tell I had settled down and accepted my "fate," she left for home. I know this because years later she told me so. But that's okay. It worked. And I was fine from there on out. At least in kindergarten, that is.

And as I mentioned earlier, there's not much else of value to say about kindergarten, or other early schooling experiences. Again, pretty typical stuff.

However, the important aspect of those experiences for me was its orientation. Roman Catholic from first through twelfth grades starting at St. Anselm's School, and continuing on to Marin Catholic High School. As if that were not enough religion, then I went for two more years at a Jesuit college. (See Exhibit II for complete education record.) Along with a Catholic upbringing that kind of education can have an indelible impact on the rest of your life.

And not always a positive one. Although there were exceptions to that including a second grade nun who I literally fell in love with from the first moment. She had an absolutely beautiful, almost angelic, face. And she was very, very kind. While I recall her, at my age my memory is not my strong suit. So, it took a while, however, but after considerable thought I finally was able to pull up her name: Sister Eulalie Rose.

Of course, I think I talked incessantly about her to my mother. Until one day when she told me, half seriously, that no, I could not marry Sister Eulalie Rose. Up to that point I was pretty much convinced that when I got a little older I would propose to Sister Eulalie Rose; we would marry each other and live a blissful life thereafter.

Silly me.

Mom cautioned me; you can't marry a nun since she is already taken, married to Our Lord, Jesus Christ. Besides, she was a good twenty plus years older than me. One day she might unfortunately die and leave me behind. Had I thought of that? That warning was a rude awakening for a seven year old who was in love. I would have to find another more realistic love interest.

As was the case with Sister Eulalie, some of my grade school teachers are more memorable than others. For example, I do remember my fourth grade teacher, Mrs. Marks. She was nowhere near as beautiful as Sister Eulalie, but she was fine. But kind of on the old side. Something stuck with me about her and I don't know if she really believed it or not, but Mrs. Marks told my parents at an open house that she wished she had "forty-eight Craigs" in her classroom. At least that's what they told me. I guess that was because there were so many kids in that classroom who were absolute terrors. So, it was all relative.

I think that was the year that I had a birthday party and all of us fourth graders went to the movie theater downtown. It was a bit of a chaotic experience for my poor mom, particularly when she had to go after one of those terrors who decided he was going to crawl around under all the theater seats.

One memory that stands out is my participation in Cub Scouts; I'm not clear on exactly when, I think it was around the age of seven or eight (Cub Scouts can range in age from five to ten years old).

That experience is particularly notable because of my bewilderment when one day at school I learned that other kids were joining a local "den" of Cub Scouts. I felt left out and expressed that feeling to my mother when I got home.

Apparently, my friend Michael's mother was the den leader and so my mom contacted her and told her I was upset at not being included. At that point we learned that the opportunity to join occurred on a day when I was home from school with a bad cold.

Next thing I knew, there I was in the Cub Scouts, working on all my "electives" to gain my first award, a "yellow feather."

Being the overachiever that I was, it turned out that I was the first of the six other Cubs to achieve that notoriety. I remember that one like it was yesterday.

But the most prominent of Cub Scout activities for me (and most certainly my mom's) occurred one Friday evening during one of our "pack" meetings (A pack is an amalgam of dens that meet monthly).

There were all manner of exercises that the Cub Scouts went through on those Friday nights. However, the one that stands out for me is the time that all of us Cubs were told to sit along the edge of the stage of the auditorium, take off our shoes and socks, after which we were all covered with a long sheet leaving only our feet exposed.

Then our mothers were asked to identify their sons based only on the appearance of their feet. It was comical because most of the moms failed this exercise, but not my mom. I was easy for her to spot since one of the toes on my right foot crossed slightly over the next toe (I think that improved over time since I no longer notice that little deformity).

When the sheet was removed, low and behold, there was Mrs. Blake correctly identifying her son Craig. And while she was quite pleased with herself, I was just a tad embarrassed because of my toes being a bit different from other kids.

That was the point in time when I started to become acutely aware of my "physicality," and how not only my toes, but also my ears, were less than perfect.

More on that later.

Another memory that stands out was my artistic ability, which others noted in the early grades. It may have been in Mrs. Marks classroom that that particular ability was first demonstrated, because at one of our recesses a couple of those terrors, one named "Frankie" and the other named "Buzz," approached me, with Frankie asking if I could draw them a picture of a naked lady? And he had the strangest leering expression on his face as he asked that question.

I didn't have a clue as to how I should handle his request, so I made some lame excuse that I needed to pee or something and then split the scene.

Speaking of Frankie, another interesting anecdote was when I ran into him almost twenty years later on a day when I was at SF State waiting for Sally, my girlfriend at the time, to meet me after her class. I recognized him sitting on a nearby bench despite his looking like he had been pumping iron ever since the fourth grade. Surprised to see him, I went over his way and said, "Hi, Frankie, how's it going?" After which he gave me an annoyed look and replied, "I don't know ya!"

I was thinking of saying, "I'm the guy from St. Anselm's who draws naked ladies," but thought better of that, instead saying, "We went to St. Anselm's years ago." At that, he merely nodded and mumbled something incomprehensible. At which point I said, "I'd like to talk but I have to pee, ha, ha." Obviously, he didn't have a clue about that remark either and was looking more and more annoyed with me. So, I decided to leave Frankie to his devices and moved on.

Another memory associated with Mrs. Mark's fourth grade was the time during a geography lesson that she asked the class: Which Ocean is larger, the Atlantic or the Pacific?

And then she asked for a show of hands. "Who thinks the Pacific is larger?" Almost the entire class raises their hands.

"Who thinks the Atlantic is larger?" Only two hands go up, mine and one belonging to a kid whose name I think was Richard Stevens. Or was it Steven Richards? I'm not sure. What I am sure of is that we were the only two who thought the Atlantic was larger. I don't know what Richard's, or Steven's, rationale was but mine was that the word Atlantic is larger than the Pacific by one letter.

Of course, I was wrong. I felt so stupid. And I wondered at that point if she still wanted forty-eight Craigs in her class.

As far as those terrors in her classroom, well, they finally met their match when they arrived at the eighth grade "doorstep" of Sister Benigna. She was a terror in her own right. She didn't take crap from anyone and enforced that with a ruler.

Uncharitably, some of her students twisted her name around in a way that suggested she was a large black person. I'm too kind to speak it myself so I'll leave that consideration to the reader.

The eighth grade is also memorable for dancing lessons that were forced on us as preparation for high school dances, I guess. All kinds of dance steps such as the Rumba, Fox Trot, etc., etc., which I never used after that. I think the only step that served me well was the good old "Box Step." That came in handy more than once in the years thereafter.

The most irritating part of these lessons was when we formed lines, boys on one side, girls on the other, and then we would eventually come together, pairing off with some partner we could never anticipate being paired with. And it seemed like every single time I was partnered with a particular girl of such girth (and who probably outweighed me by a good thirty pounds) that I couldn't get my arms around her for the life of me.

And she tended to sweat a lot on top of that. Nonetheless, I got the feeling that she was just as uncomfortable with skinny me as I was with her.

Another memory associated with eighth grade was when my friend Peter was running for student body president.

Surprisingly, when he was asked who he wanted as his campaign manager, he pointed to me and said, "I want Craig."

After the fact, I realized the reason for my appointment and it wasn't because of my political savvy of which I had none. A few weeks earlier the mother of one of my school friends had asked me to do some posters for a local bazaar because somehow she knew I had some kind of artistic ability. They turned out quite nice, I recall. In turn, Peter saw them and wanted to harness that ability for the purposes of his campaign. So, Craig becomes campaign manager, AKA "poster guy."

I have to admit, the posters I did for him also turned out quite nice. Unfortunately, they weren't nice enough for him to win the election. He went down to defeat a couple of weeks later.

I would be remiss in not addressing the likely reason for Peter's defeat. Part of the campaign process was for someone to speak to the qualities of each of the candidates; in other words, why should that candidate get the student bodies' vote?

In all cases except one, the campaign manager took on this role. And that one exception was Peter's campaign manager who chickened out at the last minute.

Later in life I would learn that I was a pretty decent speaker and had no fear whatsoever of public presentations. Unfortunately, I didn't know that in the eighth grade and informed Peter that I had "butterflies" and couldn't speak. And I told him this about five minutes before our time to explain why Peter would be such a great student body president.

So, what happened? The speech I wrote (but ended up not giving) needed to be given by Peter himself. So, everywhere in the speech that I had written, "My candidate will, blah, blah, blah," now required Peter to instead say, "I will blah, blah, blah." That did not go well as he didn't get it right every time, stumbling over certain parts of the speech as he ended up saying something like, "My candidate will, oh, excuse me, ... I will blah, blah, blah."

Actually, I thought the speech I wrote was a pretty good speech; the problem was in the delivery.

Of course, his presentation got quite a few laughs from our student audience as I cringed at his obvious embarrassment. I couldn't have felt worse than I did at that point. I had let my friend down big-time!

Four years later, Peter would run for high school student body president. This time he didn't ask me to be his campaign manager. I don't recall who he did select, however, this time Peter managed to win that election.

So much for nice posters.

Did Peter hold a grudge against me for his 8th grade campaign disaster? No, he didn't. Far from it, in fact when I asked him to autograph my 1964 yearbook four years later, he wrote, "To my eighth grade campaign manager – you were wonderful, and you still are."

Peter's background is interesting and worthy of a few more

words. Upon graduation from high school, Peter went on to my alma mater (Cal) where he earned his bachelor's degree in Zoology. As far as I know he never ran for any student offices while at Cal.

Ultimately, he received his doctorate in Biology from Boston University. He is now a successful horticulturalist and botanist and teaches in the Harvard School of Design, championing the use of Ginkgo Biloba in an urban setting. Interestingly, he substitutes the word "spontaneous," as opposed to "invasive," when discussing urban flora which some people see as "weeds." He won't use that term.

I read that he studied Ginkgoes in China for several years. And while the derivatives of that plant are used for cognitive purposes as a memory aid, Peter is skeptical of its capability in that regard. He suggests that the concept as an effective health agent began in the board room of a German company in the 1960s, and has resulted in being a big "cash cow."

I don't believe Peter runs for office anymore. Although there may be some associated with his horticulturist profession that I haven't heard about.

St. Anselm's brings back other memories. During my time there, I served as an altar boy at St. Anselm's Church. Originally, I had been somewhat apprehensive about doing that. My brother had been an altar boy, however, and I guess I thought I should continue in that tradition.

I read that the notion of an "altar boy" first came about in

1938, when Father Benz, a priest in the archdiocese of St. Paul, Minnesota, formed the society of altar boys. That's interesting for more than one reason. One of those being that my father was born and raised near St. Paul, Minnesota, in a city named Pierz.

I don't think I ever asked my dad whether he had been an altar boy. However, given the fact that he would have been twenty-seven years old in the year 1938, he probably couldn't have been one.

When confronted with the opportunity to be an altar boy, however, I was somewhat anxious. The main reason I was apprehensive about it was because my brother Reid told me it wasn't all that difficult; I would just need to learn "the movements."

I wasn't all that clear about those movements. But I did observe that some altar boys like my brother, when they were kneeling at the altar, would sway back and forth. Of course, I thought these were "the movements" I'd need to learn. So, I continued to observe altar boys every time I was at church. But I eventually found that they didn't all sway back and forth. Or at least not in the same way. Some just knelt with absolutely no swaying motion. Others would sway one way but not always the other. And so on and so forth.

I convinced myself that I could never be an altar boy since I would not know when I should sway and in what direction.

Finally, and because I was too embarrassed to ask my brother, I talked to someone a little older. I don't recall who he was. But when I brought up the subject of "movements" to this person, and my interpretation of them, he started laughing and couldn't stop.

I failed to see the humor about this concern of mine. At which point the person told me that the movements my brother referred to involved where to go and what to do when you got there. As in going to get the wine for the priest. It had absolutely nothing to do with any kind of swaying motion. All that indicated was the degree to which a given altar boy was uncomfortable kneeling there, and was trying to aleve that discomfort by swaying back and forth a bit.

How interesting! Now I could apply to be an altar boy without stressing out over it. And that was fortuitous because every year the altar boys would get to go to a place I heard as being "Boys Hot Springs." I was told that that experience was a lot of fun because there was a large swimming pool and also an arcade area with all kinds of games to play.

When I first arrived at Boys Hot Springs, however, I wondered who "the boys" were and where were they?

Once again, something got lost in the translation. There were no "boys" already there because the place was named "Boyd's Hot Springs," not "Boys Hot Springs."

As my partner Rhonda would note many years later, I really need to get my hearing checked out!

2 - Blakes All the Way Down

Like any child, one day I asked my parents where I came from. I think for me that was at about age six or seven. Obviously, I was a little too young for my mom or dad to talk about sex in all its aspects.

Now, I had a theory that parents had kids somehow, someway, but I was not clear as to what that process entailed. My theory went on to speculate that some people, like my parents, were "born big." After all, how would us kids come about if they weren't?

I was going to share my theory with my parents until one day when they answered my question about where I came from. I believe the answer provided by my mom was something like I came from "The Blakes" and "The Reids."

Although that didn't really answer my question, I think I said at that point, "Where did they come from, Mom?"

That was probably the first time I recall being told that, "The Blakes came from Minnesota," and, "The Reids came from Vallejo."

So, focusing on my Dad's side I asked something like, "Where did The Blakes come from before they were in Minnesota?"

It now got a little more complicated. I was told they came from Germany, but my father said that their family wasn't always named "Blake."

So, I asked him what their names were before. He said that they were originally named "Block," but they changed their name when they came to our country.

I asked, "Why did they do that?"

I was then told that mean people called them "block heads."

Well, that was interesting in and of itself, I thought. And it caused me to want to know more about our family, and what was referred to as "our family tree."

Dad proceeded to tell me that my grandparents on the Blake side were named "Jacob" and "Adelaide." My grandmother had only recently passed away, but he wasn't so sure about his father. He didn't say anymore after that.

If my memory serves me correctly, later I learned from my mom that Jacob Blake abandoned his wife and eleven children. Wow! Eleven children! He did the deed and then took off!

I don't recall if my mom told me the names of my grandparents on her side, however. She did tell me that, sadly, her own mother died when my mom was only twelve years old. I don't think she told me how her mom died. Somewhere along the line I learned that her father was named Albert. He was still alive for a very few years when I was a toddler. And I believe my parents took care of him until he passed on.

Because I was so young, I recall almost nothing about Grandmother Adelaide or Grandfather Albert. Again, that "infant amnesia" Freud talked about.

Beyond that information, I didn't look into my family tree at that time. Many years later, however, when Elena and I had our grandchild, Eli, on my son Jeffrey's side, I became more curious about our ancestry. So, I used two Web sites, Ancestry.com and 23&me.com, which Rhonda had gifted me with, to garner more background information on our family.

In the process of checking out these Web sites, I became acquainted with a lady named Ellen Blake (not her maiden name), who is married to Ken Blake, and has done quite a bit of Blake family research herself. She had managed to trace our lineage back as far as the year 1742, almost two hundred and eighty years ago.

If her information was correct, there may never have been a "Block" name to begin with. I couldn't ask my Dad about that since he was unfortunately not alive at the time, so I concluded that either he was joking about the family name, or he was seriously misinformed about it.

Nonetheless, there are at least a couple of theories about the "Blake vs. Block" conundrum. One theory, proposed by Ellen Blake herself, supports my father's observation, that is, depending on where you look, the Blake name has shown up in various German records as "Bleck." And it has also appeared as "Blek," "Black," "Block," "Blik," "Blak," and "Blake," in various census records.

The other theory is held by a Mrs. Otten who believes that the Blake name is the correct name, and that our predecessors came from Ireland. However, this is merely a theory and is not supported by any available records.

Armed with the information that Ellen Blake provided me, I learned that my great-great-great-great grandparents were Michael and Maria Blake, not Block. And so on. Blakes all the way down.

Michael and Maria married in February of 1767 in Kradenbach, Germany. They lived in Bongard, Germany. They had two children, Nicholas and John. This was referred to as "Generation No. 1," according to the information provided by Ellen Blake.

There is no information on Nicholas; however, the lineage continues on with the other son, John, marrying Anna Roden, and they had two children as well, both girls. They married in Steinenberg, Germany. And apparently John married a second time. His second wife's name was Marie Schroeder, and that marriage bore six children, five boys and one girl.

It is unclear why John married a second time, but had he not, the Blake lineage might have stopped there since his first marriage bore only girls.

What is notable at this time is that the five sons all were born in Germany, but moved to America, living in the states of Iowa, Illinois, and Minnesota.

The generations continue after that with my grandparents, Jacob and Adelaide (Generation No. Five) giving birth to eleven children, five sons and six daughters. One child died at a very young age. I don't know what she died of.

The sons included my father, Reinhart, who was born on April 6, 1911, in Minnesota. I believe the city was Pierz.

I have streamlined the information provided by Ellen Blake, and updated it with Generation Nos. 6 through 8, which is provided in Exhibit I. Note that the lineage addresses only direct descendants.

My father moved from Minnesota to California, where he met and married my mother, Grace Ann Reid, on May 28, 1939. I'm embarrassed to admit it, but I didn't recall the exact date of their marriage. So, I had to do some digging but was eventually able to pull up that date. They eventually moved from Vallejo to San Anselmo, both in California.

What is a bit interesting is that while my brother Reid was born just over a year later, I took another five plus years to arrive. For whatever reason, more than one person questioned that delay. Without some form of birth control, that doesn't happen very often, I guess.

Maybe it was a little of that infamous "German stubbornness" (which I will discuss in an upcoming episode) in me that caused the five year hiatus.

3 - The Vallejo Connection

I'll discuss my immediate family in the following episodes, but before that I should address the "Vallejo connection," which continued on over time.

While I was still quite young, I recall our family making what I would call "pilgrimages" to the city of Vallejo just about every Sunday, the only day of the week that my dad wasn't working. Now maybe it just seemed like we traveled there every Sunday, I'm not quite sure. But I do have vivid memories of riding across the marshes along Highway 37 between Marin County and Vallejo.

And I also recall my dad suggesting that on Sunday we go to an early Mass "to get it over with." I don't think he meant it the way it sounded; he just wanted to get a leg up on it in case we were making one of those pilgrimages to Vallejo.

So, off we went to 9:15 am Mass, which was actually the Mass that St. Anselm's students would attend. I believe I sat in the required locale with my "colleagues," while my parents sat elsewhere. Afterwards we'd make small talk outside the church with the folks leaving Mass and sometimes with the priest who had presided over Mass.

And then we might head off to Vallejo.

Those trips were memorable in more than one way. Of course that Highway 37 road with its marshes which seemed to go on and on was certainly part of that memory.

My grandmother, Adelaide Blake, was alive and living in Vallejo until her death in 1950. Since I was only three or four years old at the time, I really can't remember her at all.

However, a couple of years later, maybe around 1952 or 1953, I escaped from that "infant amnesia" I've been talking about. From that point on, I do recall what I now refer to as that Vallejo connection.

That involved the various stops at relatives' homes and, in one case, the business of one of those relatives. It seemed like we would always go to my Aunt Chris's place first. I think her full name was Christine, but don't quote me on that. Her home was memorable because there was a nice park down the street from her place and oftentimes I would go to that park to play on the swings and climb the monkey bars.

Also at her home was her husband, Herman, who happened to be my Godfather. He was almost always sitting in the back yard drinking a beer. Uncle Herman and I would have long, somewhat tedious talks. I say "tedious" because he always told me we would go to a lake to fish for Bass. But we never did. Nonetheless, I still liked Uncle Herman.

After Aunt Chris's stop we would sometimes go to her son's store in Vallejo. I think it was closed most of the time, but he was still there doing I don't know what. We called him "Junior" because his name was Herman too. He seemed like a nice guy.

From Junior's place our path was not always consistent. Sometimes we would go to Lucille and Jack's place. Lucille was the daughter of Pierce Porter and Kathryn Blake Porter and she was married more than once. I think her first husband was called "Jocko." Interesting name: it probably stood for something else like "Jack," I really don't know. In any case, when we went there we also visited with her current husband, who was also named Jack. I guess she really liked that name.

Now I thought that Jack was a pretty neat guy. He also happened to be a fireman, and he always had interesting stories to tell. However, years later my cousin Cece (Bless her soul) would tell me that he wasn't really the type of person I thought he was. She didn't go into details but clearly she had a different opinion of the man who was actually her stepfather.

Again, our paths weren't always consistent; however, after the last visit with Lucille and Jack, oftentimes we would travel on to my mom's side of the family to visit Aunt Alice who was my mom's sister. She lived in a very nice, almost historic-looking, house in another area of town. It might have been on Tennessee Street. Many of the streets in Vallejo were named after states.

In any case, I really liked Aunt Alice; one reason might be that she always remembered my birthday, and would send me a card with five dollars in it. That may not sound like a lot of money, but in the 1950s it was not a paltry amount. In terms of today's dollars, that would be equivalent to over fifty dollars. And to top it off, she was retired from her job at "the Arsenal," in Vallejo, which was a facility of the U.S. Army I believe. So, she was living on whatever pension she had.

I had another aunt, Aunt Helen, who lived with Aunt Alice for a time but eventually she married a guy named "Bub," (or was it "Bud"?) and moved in with him. Aunt Helen was actually what you would call a "spinster" prior to that. And I think they lived in a large trailer but don't quote me on that either.

What was interesting about Bub or Bud, was that he had a type of dog called a Weimaraner, which is a rather large canine. I don't recall the name of that Weimaraner, however.

So, back to Aunt Alice. She was married at one time, but not when we visited. I don't recall her husband's name, but his last name must have been "Speck," since she was "Aunt Alice Speck." No one talked about him; there must have been something not particularly good about this guy.

In any case, we would sit and chat with Aunt Alice who also liked to drink beer. She and Uncle Herman would have gotten along very well. But, of course, he was already taken. Our visits there weren't very long since the day was getting on at that point.

I enjoyed those trips for many reasons, but the most important was we just about always ended the journey with a stop at a place called "Lloyd's Restaurant." It had a lot of charm as I recall. And I would always get a hot turkey sandwich there since that was my favorite dinner.

Sometimes on our trip to Vallejo we would also drive over to Napa to visit with my "Uncle Billy." He wasn't really my uncle but my cousin; he was also a son of Herman and Chris. But I think I called him that because he was a good thirty years older than me.

The interesting thing about Uncle Billy was his ownership of a billiards parlor. He would always be there when we visited on a Sunday. I probably should have asked him to show me how to shoot billiards, which is similar to pool except I think it doesn't have "pockets."

Like his brother Herman, Billy was a smooth talker. I don't mean that in a negative way. He just seemed to be able to carry on a pretty nice conversation when we visited and my parents seemed to like him.

I don't recall a lot about Junior or Billy's families. I do recall that Billy was married to a very nice lady named Pauline. And Herman was married to a lady named Carol. They had a daughter named Vickie who I still keep in touch with through the electronic medium.

That's about it for our "Vallejo Connection," although I may refer back to it in future episodes.

4 - This Cat Has No Tail!

Both my brother Reid and I were born in Marin County. Reid was born in 1941, a bit more than five years ahead of me.

And the first home that I remember, although one other home proceeded it, was located on Morningside Drive in San Anselmo. Before a disaster (which I will shortly describe) occurred at that address, my brother and I really enjoyed life there. There was a big hill down the street which we scaled once just to see what was on the other side. It must not have been memorable, however, since I don't recall what was there.

And Morningside Drive was the first home where I had a pet cat. His name was "Prince" because he absolutely looked like royalty. At least to me.

I would go on to have at least three more felines including one named "Pepper," one named "Snicker," and another whose name I don't recall but was distinguished by one little anomaly which I first realized as my parents and I drove home from Mill Valley where we got him.

It went like this. We all got into the car, I with my new cat in the back seat. We continued on, driving over the hill that separates Mill Valley from Corte Madera. When we were almost halfway up that hill I remember something like it was only yesterday. I took one look at the behind of my feline only to shout to my parents, "This cat has no tail!"

To which my mom calmly replied, "It's okay, Craig; we'll check him out when we get home."

As it turned out, we first thought that the cat was a Manx, which can have a short stubby tail. On closer inspection, we noted a little kink in the tail, like the tail had gotten caught into something and all it had left was this little kink. We weren't really sure.

In hindsight, I think we should have called the former owners and asked about it. But we didn't. Because I really liked the cat otherwise and didn't want to return him.

I wish I could remember the name we gave him. I think it related to his tail (like "Stubby"?), but I'm not sure of that.

In any case, I have many fond memories of living on Morningside Drive. One of them is a nice older lady, who lived nearby, who I'll call Mrs. Sabatini. My mom visited her frequently and when I joined her, Mrs. Sabatini would always offer me a coke to drink. I recall that she literally had crates of them available inside her garage. In later years I would learn that Mrs. Sabatini drank a lot and that her drink of choice was rum and coke. That may also explain why she always seemed so happy.

Another nice memory related to the big oak tree in the corner of our large back yard. Of course when one has a large oak tree, one needs to have a tree house in it. And so Reid and I, with considerable help from our father, built one. It was a rather large tree house which could accommodate the two of us and one or two friends. So we decided we needed a name for our tree house. At that time we had come into possession of a small red stapler, called a "Swingline Tot." Although it had nothing to do with the treehouse, we decided to call our place "Big Tot."

There are many other memories of Morningside. There were two kids down the street who I'll refer to as the "Sadowski brothers," and they always seemed to be getting into trouble of all types. I think my mom wanted me to have nothing to do with them, but we still hung out with them.

And there was a boy, who I will call Todd, who was a few years older than me, but younger than Reid who Reid "pantsed" one day. (That means he pulled his pants down around his ankles.) And it was such an embarrassing episode for Todd that we never saw him much after that. Poor Todd.

One more memory of my time at Morningside. I took the bus to St. Anselm's School every school day. The driver of the bus was a big guy named "Sam Something," and he happened to also be the police chief for San Anselmo, so nobody gave him any guff.

For some reason, these bus rides were always memorable. I recall one time in particular. I had a cousin (who I won't identify) who lived down the street. For whatever reason, everyone made fun of her. (That was not very nice and I didn't join in.) So it was particularly annoying that she would go around telling other kids that I was her cousin, which of course I always denied.

One day on the school bus, while she was trying to get to her seat, the bus jerked (I don't know why) and she went flying down to the front doors of the bus, landing upside down with her dress exposing her to some degree. Of course everyone laughed at that, but I didn't. I felt very sorry for her at that point.

To make up for it, after that I didn't deny I was her cousin anymore.

And while I'm speaking of my cousin, I will briefly return to the lineage described earlier (See "Blakes All the Way Down"). The ancestry reports revealed several interesting facts including the composition of my ancestors such that the British and Irish component was 67.8%, French and German was 20.8%, with Scandinavian at 3.2%, and the remaining 8.2% spread across Europe.

Some other interesting tidbits regarding my origins as follows:

I'm likely not to have a "bald spot." I find this very interesting since my father, and all his brothers I believe, had bald spots. Even my brother Reid had a bit of a bald spot.

Related to that was that there was little likelihood of

early hair loss, although my father and brother exhibited that characteristic.

I could relate to the fact that I would be more likely than average to be fearful of heights.

I could also relate to preferring sweets to salty foods.

And here's an interesting tidbit. I seem to have some connection with my Neanderthal ancestors who have difficulty discarding rarely used possessions.

That could well be.

Also, I am at a slightly increased risk of having what is called "Celiac Disease." Since I don't have any idea what that is about, I looked it up. It's an immune reaction to eating gluten that creates inflammation resulting in damage to the small intestine lining leading to medical complications. The classic symptom is diarrhea. Other symptoms can include bloating gas, fatigue and low blood count.

Although I'm merely at "slightly increased risk," I looked for possible treatments and found that the mainstay was a strict gluten-free diet, which makes sense.

I don't seem to have markers for any other significant diseases.

That's good. I hope they're right about that, however.

5 - Shot for Boy in Room Twelve!

Most of my life I've been fairly healthy, but with a few bumps along the way.

I'll get to those exceptions as we progress through this part of the memoir about my early life.

As with many children of that age, I had a case of tonsilitis around age seven. And perhaps it was the second most fearful event up to that point in my life after the kindergarten experience.

What echoes in my mind about this particular experience are the words, "Shot for boy in room twelve!"

Oh, yes, "Shot for boy in room twelve!"

Although I've included an exclamation point at the end of that sentence, it wasn't necessarily shouted. Rather it's my own way of injecting the kind of fear I felt inside me when I heard those words being uttered by a nurse from down the hallway in the hospital when I was taken there for my tonsillectomy.

It seems hard to believe, but as I recall the experience sixty-seven years later, those words were uttered multiple times. Why would I have had to have that many shots? Or did I hear it only once, but it was so inherently fearful that it only seemed to be repeated over and over?

I really don't know.

And I wasn't one to readily accept things, even at the tender age of seven. So when the nurse finally arrived to administer that shot and told me something like, "Doctor Smith (or whoever) wants you to have this shot," I would resist, saying that was not my doctor. "My doctor is Dr. Whatchamacallit (I don't remember his name)," I insisted.

And her retort was something like, "Dr. Smith is the doctor on duty right now, and he wants you to have this shot very, very much."

So I was shot regardless of my resistance.

It seemed at the time that I was in that hospital, which was named the Ross Cottage Hospital, for an eternity whereas it was probably more like two days.

What I do know for sure is how relieved I was when I was finally told it was time to go home.

And an added bonus when I got there. I was lavished with presents of all kinds, including my favorite: a Charley McCarthy dummy! If you haven't heard of this dummy, he was first named by the ventriloquist fellow, Edgar Bergen. He started in radio and then went to television. McCarthy was one of two Bergen dummies, the other being named Mortimer Snerd.

While there were toy Charlie McCarthy dummies that could be purchased, I don't think there were any Mortimer Snerds.

In any case, that trip to the hospital was finally paying off!

As I noted earlier, I've had relatively good health with a "few bumps along the way." One of those bumps occurred when Elena and I lived in our first house on Shady Draw in Pinole.

At the time I was about 29 years of age and felt pretty good health-wise, that was until one day when Elena was out shopping and I was relaxing as I read the newspaper. Out of the blue, whamo, my heart began to race. Ultimately, it was clocked in at more than 170 beats per minute. And it didn't seem like it wanted to stop.

In a panic, I ran across the street to a friendly neighbor's house. He was on his front lawn doing some gardening, I think. I told him I thought I was having a heart attack and asked him if he would take me to a local hospital that was only about five minutes away. He accommodated me and we were then off to the emergency ward.

I vividly recall him driving about five miles an hour under the speed limit. Or maybe it just seemed like that. So, I asked if he would please drive a bit faster.

I thought I was having a heart attack which I was not. But it certainly felt like that. Eventually we arrived at emergency, and we went inside. I think they took me in relatively quickly when I told them I thought I was having something heart-related.

Long story short, I wasn't having a heart attack, but I was experiencing a form of tachycardia referred to as atrial fibrillation. I read that such a rapid heart rate is caused by chaotic, irregular electrical impulses in the upper chambers of the heart. Such signals result in rapid, uncoordinated, and weak contractions of the atria.

There are more serious forms of tachycardia, primarily one called ventricular fibrillation, in which long episodes can be life-threatening.

So, I was relieved, of course, that I wasn't experiencing a more serious condition involving an impeded blood flow to my heart, a condition which could lead to death. However, I would soon realize that this wasn't a one-time occurrence. It would continue, off and on, to the point that ultimately a Kaiser physician would prescribe what is called a "beta blocker" designed to mitigate any reoccurrence of the condition.

There were also situations wherein my heart beat in an irregular fashion. While the beta blockers helped to eliminate the tachycardia, it didn't seem to eliminate those situations, but with time they became less and less frequent.

I continued with the beta blockers, some different from others, for many years thereafter until one day, almost magically, the condition disappeared completely. I can't say when exactly that happened. It has now been quite a while.

However, I was very relieved when I got to the point that I no longer required beta blockers.

Another "bump" along the road of good health, occurred sometime after I was prescribed the drug Suboxone (which I will discuss more fully a little later), but wasn't necessarily related to it. I was being treated for pneumonia since September of 2008, and ultimately was hospitalized due to this particular form of pneumonia which occurs when food particles are stuck in the lungs.

During that time, I was prescribed as many as fourteen different medications and saw multiple doctors. I also had a hiatal hernia for which I had corrective surgery called laparoscopic fundoplication. I hasten to add that, despite its name, there's nothing "fun" about it.

I was hospitalized for several days, more than once, at a Burlingame hospital. And during one of those stays, I learned from a nurse that my heart stopped beating during a trip in the elevator.

These clearly were not good times for me, health-wise. I eventually took time off from my teaching position for purposes of recuperation.

While I was able to return to my teaching duties eventually, it was on a part-time basis, and in June 2010, I retired from my position as professor at the College of San Mateo.

I'll talk more about my "professorial work" later on.

6 - My Parents' Nightmare

Let's return to that earlier era when my family lived on Morningside Drive, noting that while it is not easy to pull up those long-term memories at my age, some things just stick with me as I grow older. The best example of that is the day, when I was very young, that the "bulkhead" broke.

"What is a bulkhead?" you ask.

A lesson in civil engineering is appropriate at this stage. A bulkhead can take many forms, but in this case it refers to a retaining wall that supports the landscape next to a creek. If it were not there, under certain conditions the landscape could collapse into the creek.

Here's how this story goes.

My parents bought their first (and last as it turned out) house when I was about five years old. This house was located in a very nice section of San Anselmo, California, earlier noted as Morningside Drive. I think it cost about $14,000 at the time, not an insignificant amount by the standards of that day. According to zillow.com, today it would sell for a tad below $2 million.

Although my father managed a grocery store at that point in his life, he was also a skilled carpenter by avocation. So he threw himself into making improvements to the structure including a work shop on the bottom floor. And with that workshop came more improvements including a large all-purpose room on the same floor complete with a kitchen and bathroom. I seem to recall that we referred to the large room as a "rumpus" room. You don't hear that designation much anymore.

But he didn't stop there. He worked long hours every day, six days a week, but he still found time during his limited off-hours to build a very large deck at the back of the house, which looked out over the back yard landscape.

My brother Reid and I helped him with that project wherein it was necessary to drill holes into the concrete structure supporting the deck. I don't know why, but I clearly remember that that activity took us quite a while to complete.

In any case, after considerable effort on everyone's part, we had a wonderful redwood decking, which was painted, with stairs leading up to it. I remember the good times we had having barbeques and other activities on that deck. However, we were not destined to enjoy those activities for very long. During the winter of 1955, there was a ferocious storm, a storm of the century they called it at the time. And San Anselmo had long been known for its severe flooding along its creeks and streams.

So here's the civil engineering part of the story. Our bulkhead was built with redwood, the way it was supposed to be. However, our stupid neighbor built his bulkhead with concrete, and it wasn't very well built to begin with. That ferocious storm ended up taking his bulkhead down and with that it took ours down as well.

As a result, one morning we looked out the back windows of our house only to see half of our very large backyard sunk into the creek. Under the circumstances there was no way we could have prevented that outcome. It goes without saying that there was considerable cost involved in hiring a civil engineering firm to come in, fill up our backyard again, and then build a new bulkhead. I recall the name of the contractor, Mr. Servante, who undertook the work. I'm not positive of this fact, but I believe he quoted my father the cost of the work amounting to almost half the price of the house itself.

My parents did everything they could to mitigate the costs of construction, including hiring a lawyer, and going to the city council (I'm not sure what the point of that exercise was all about). And they undoubtedly lost a lot of sleep over all of this.

Despite all of their efforts, in the end they had to eat the entire cost themselves.

Shortly thereafter they put the house up for sale. I'm not sure why; I think that the place just had too many negative memories at that point. Or maybe they were afraid that the replacement bulkhead would itself fail one day.

As I said earlier, this was the first and also the last house they owned. We looked for another house in the San Anselmo area after that. Because of my dad's job and also my attendance at St. Anselm's School, my parents wanted to stay in or near San Anselmo.

I recall a Spanish style home in an area called Sleepy Hollow that I thought was really neat and hoped we would buy it. But when my dad saw a sump pump in the basement, that was the death nell of that particular abode. Sump pumps mean that basements flood and need to have the water pumped out. At this point my father had a real aversion to anything that involved water, which was understandable.

And I remember another house we looked at on a nice shady street in San Anselmo. The street even had an appropriate name: Prospect Avenue. But that particular "prospect" was not for us because my father said that the steep hill behind it might find itself sluffing off into the house during another potentially bad winter.

There were others as well, too numerous to name, but it seemed like every single one posed a hazard of one nature or another. My dad was a smart man, who was also a cautious man, not ready for another disastrous winter that would do our next house in.

We looked and we looked, but long story short, my parents decided that it would be wiser at this point in our lives not to buy the next residence. Let someone else take on the legal responsibilities associated with home ownership. So they ended up renting a nice older home on Greenfield Avenue, again in San Anselmo. For one reason or another that house didn't have the same positive vibes (before that winter obviously) that the home on Morningside Drive had.

As a matter of fact, there were quite a few negative vibes associated with Greenfield Avenue. It was during the time we lived there that my folks would begin to experience a falling out with my brother (more on that later) and yet another nightmare experience for my father.

It was also disconcerting that my parents seemed to argue more at the Greenfield address than they did in the past. I'm not even sure what those arguments were about but when they occurred, they were ferocious. And oftentimes my mom would cry and then end up sleeping on the living room sofa. I felt sorry for her and didn't know how to comfort her when this happened.

Later in life I would learn that after such arguments, most wives get to sleep in the bedroom at night, and that husbands are the ones who are relegated to the couch.

That's another story, however.

7 - Yet Another Nightmare

My father was devoted to his job as a grocery store manager with an outfit called "Purity Stores." He had started working for that enterprise in a Vallejo store, after which he was transferred to the San Anselmo location as the store manager. Eventually, there was stiff competition from other markets in the town, mainly Safeway, with the resulting closure of my dad's store. More on that later.

But there were some positive memories associated with that locale on Tunstead Avenue. My dad let me help him in the storeroom with deliveries of goods. I vividly remember those large railing systems with coasters (What do they call those?) through which boxes came flying into the storeroom.

That was fun.

And I remember the many times that I would use my dad's store as a "base of operations" for trips to the barber shop, the soda fountain at Jack's Drug Store down the street (Yes, there really were soda fountains in those days), the local theater and, of course my favorite, a large toy store just a few blocks away.

San Anselmo was a really neat town. At Christmas, the local fire department across the street from the store had a nativity scene and then one year a flying Santa Claus in a plane going around the flag pole (Or did I dream that?).

I also recall my "carpenter father" building a staircase and observation area in the store so that he could see what was going on while he was away from the checkout areas. He was very diligent, and a serious minded manager at that. Nonetheless, I could also tell that his subordinates and others that he worked with really liked him. I remember some of their names: there was an older lady named Mable, and there was an Irishman named Timmy, and a man named Frank who came to take inventories with my dad.

There's a little story there as well. One year when my dad was very busy and didn't have time to leave the store, he asked "Inventory Frank" if he gave him some money would he be good enough to buy my mother some nice Samsonite luggage for her upcoming birthday.

I don't know why he had him buy that luggage since my parents rarely went anywhere. There were some vacations we took as a family, the most elaborate of which was a cross country trip to my father's homeland in Minnesota. But that was much earlier than the luggage purchase. Ironically, I think the only time my mother actually got to use that luggage was to go to Marin General Hospital to have a tumor removed. Fortunately, my mom's tumor was successfully removed, and she eventually lived to be eighty-two years old.

In any case, when my mom learned that my dad didn't buy the luggage himself, but had Inventory Frank buy it, she was livid. If I were her I don't know how I would react, but it seemed a little over the top from my viewpoint at the time.

Back to the nightmare.

It's an all too familiar story. A man devoting himself to his job who's cast aside. And so it was with my dad. After giving his all to the Purity Stores for many years, working day and night, and weekends, they decided to close his store and let him go when the competition with the nearby Safeway store argued for that closure. Of course, they did offer him a job as a checker at a store nowhere near us. That would have been pretty hard on our family. I probably would have had to give up my parochial school education and there would be other concessions our family would need to make.

And we really wanted to stay in an area where we had roots and attachments if we could.

I know my dad was hopeful that he would find himself a suitable job; however, at his age of fifty years, the pickings were few and far between. So, it was decided that he would "buy into" his next job. And with that began an odyssey in and of itself.

There was a general store (Yes, they still had those at the time, but they were largely in remote environments) in Alturas, California. In case you haven't heard of Alturas, it is situated almost at the border with Oregon, with a population of about 2,200 at the time.

My mother, bless her heart, nipped that one in the bud when she learned I'd have to take a bus to school many miles away every day.

I sort of liked that idea, but mom knew best. So, no general store for us.

Next, there was a toy store (not the one down the street from my dad's store) in neighboring Corte Madera and this one my mother really liked, thinking that this would be a natural for me when she or my dad would tell customers that they would need to "see the boy in the back" to help them with their particular purchase.

This time my dad nixed this one when he looked into the finances of this operation.

And there were many other "prospects" along the way.

In time, however, the best prospects were just too "pricey" for my parents. A decision was made that the only realistic opportunity would be one which involved other partners who would share in the financial investment.

Long story short as I like to say, my dad finally found his next "job opportunity" by joining with his brother and their nephew in the purchase of a small supermarket in Santa Venetia, an enclave just outside of San Rafael. It is noteworthy that across the street from the market, a modernistic civic center as well as a post office, both designed by the firm of the renowned architect, Frank Lloyd Wright, would be completed just two years later.

In any case, the purchase of the market ticked many of the boxes for my parents.

I could continue to attend Marin Catholic High School, in Kentfield.

There was suitable housing for us since the former owners of the store - the Santa Venetia Supermarket – rented out their former home, which was conveniently located behind the market, so my dad had a "commute" of about one hundred yards. That way he could come home for both lunch, and dinner when he worked late.

An added bonus: my mom took over the responsibility for a small contracted-out post office in the store itself with the same short commute as my father's, of course. (Ultimately, it would be replaced by the Frank Lloyd Wright structure.)

Most importantly, my dad was doing something that he liked and was good at. This brought much harmony to a family which had gone through a lot of grief over the past several years including major surgery for both parents, the "bulkhead" experience, a growing tension between my parents and my brother Reid, all of which culminated with my father's job loss.

And lastly, the arguments my parents had had become a thing of the past. There was a renewed sense of harmony between my mom and my dad.

That harmony, however, would be put to the test when tensions arose between "two stubborn Germans."

8 - Two Stubborn Germans

While there was harmony in our immediate family with my dad's purchase of the supermarket, everything was not so rosy between my dad and his partner brother.

There began a strained relationship between them after only a brief time as partners. The two were very much like each other. My mother would characterize them as "two stubborn Germans." Each of them believed he knew the best way of doing something and would not accommodate any conflicting opinions. And they had a major communication problem.

I think they must have studied under Frederick Taylor, the father of scientific management, who coined the term "the one best way." (This is a joke!)

Interestingly, there was a prevailing notion at the time that Western Germans were stubborn and taciturn. And there's a joke that fits that description as follows: A Westphalian walks through Cologne. A parrot is sitting on his shoulder. A Cologne local comes up to him and asks, "Can he talk?" The parrot responds, "How should I know?"

While they were alike in many respects, the brothers were poles apart in other ways. As an example, my dad liked a nice clean uncluttered checkout counter whereas my uncle loved to load up that counter with various impulse items, largely being candy. So my uncle would load up the counter with stuff only to have my father remove all the stuff later when he wasn't around. This went back and forth for some time. Neither wanted to accommodate the other's approach.

It all came to a head one day early on in the partnership arrangement when my dad went to drink his coffee which had been out on the counter itself. Unbeknownst to dad, his brother had poured detergent into the cup. There was a loud noise as my father spit out his coffee and yelled something incomprehensible. (This is all coming second hand since I heard the story from my mother who happened to be present at the time.)

The next thing you know, my uncle is laughing at his silly stunt and my father is racing down the aisle and physically attacking his brother. My mother than screamed out as others ran toward them, attempting to extricate the two brothers.

It was about as bad a situation as anyone could have imagined. Fortunately, no punches landed and neither brother was injured. The fallout was not physical; it was totally emotional.

The fallout from that encounter? Neither brother would speak to the other from that day forward.

How do you manage an operation when two of three partners don't communicate with each other?

That's where my cousin, the nephew of the two brothers, comes into play. Each partner had a specialty and the cousin's was the liquor area, which was appropriate for more than one reason. And it would be an understatement to say that that cousin (who I will not name) was not the hardest worker of the three partners. There were times when he was gone to who knows where and other times where his most strenuous activity was dusting off the liquor bottles in his area, which he was quite proud of.

However, after the skirmish between the two brothers, my cousin was called upon for a new and much more important role, one that I would characterize as "Chief Executive Communicator." Since the brothers would not talk to each other, someone would have to be the go-between. So, that became the nephew's function from there on out.

And while that may sound fortuitous, there were always questions whether the nephew was being completely honest about what one brother vis-à-vis the other was saying. Apparently, the brothers were willing to accept that new status quo since neither had any desire to talk to the other.

And so that went on for the next fifteen years until the day that my father finally retired from the business. And I have to say that those weren't the best years for my dad as well as my mom.

My dad's retirement brought on some good things, but also one bad thing.

One of the big pluses was that my father, along with my mother, could now have some time to spend with their new grandbaby when Elena gave birth to our first son, Matthew. Although they already had two grandsons which were products of my brother Reid and his wife Gina, the fallout between my parents and Reid now precluded any kind of relations with those two boys, Scott and Steven.

That was very sad. But now they had a grandson they could spoil.

Unfortunately, my dad was only able to hold Matthew in his arms once or twice.

This was a time when dad began to notice strange dark spots on his arms and other places in his anatomy. He consulted his doctor who assured him that it was not of a cancerous nature, probably something called Lupus, an inflammatory disease. While it is a somewhat serious condition, there are treatments available to mitigate it.

My dad was a well-informed man who read quite a bit when he had the time. He politely suggested to his doctor that he was fearful his condition presented as a form of leukemia. The doctor dismissed that, telling him not to worry.

This situation went on for a prolonged period until the point wherein further tests were performed and with those test results available, his doctor told my dad that he was right, he did have leukemia. I remember this since I was present on that day, and I asked my father's doctor whether the leukemia was chronic or acute. I had done my own research on the leukemia condition. I knew that chronic leukemia was slow moving and that acute leukemia was rapidly progressing and results in the accumulation of immature, functionless blood cells in the bone marrow. People with chronic leukemia can live many years after developing the disease. Such is not the case with the acute form of the disease.

In answer to my question, the physician told us it was the acute form. And although the doctor did not say it, I knew at that point my dad didn't have long to live, maybe a few months at best.

Despite his being a well-informed individual, I'm not sure whether my father grasped the severity of the situation when he asked his own question, "I'm thinking of buying some property near a lake. Do you ...?"

Before my dad even finished the sentence, the doctor said he should probably put that purchase on hold for the time being. It was his way of telling dad he would never be able to set foot on that property.

Well before the tests even indicated he had the disease, my dad thought he had leukemia. This was one of the rare times when my father wished he hadn't been right, but he was.

He would never retire on that lake.

9 - The Trouble with Girlfriends

As earlier noted, I was fortunate to continue my high school education at Marin Catholic High School (MCHS) after my dad had gone into the market partnership with his brother and nephew. And there was nothing particularly exceptional about the next four years for me.

However, this was a period of time when my parents and my brother Reid continued their strained relations, most of which had to do with my brother's choice of girlfriends. To be clear on this point, there wasn't anything terrible-awful about his choices. It had more to do with conflicts between my mother and the girlfriends. And I really can't put my finger on the "why" of these conflicts; they just naturally evolved over time.

I recall two or three of Reid's girlfriends, particularly Betsy and Penny, prior to his meeting and marrying his future wife, Gina.

I think my mom was down on Betsy because she came from the "boonies" up in Nicasio, which is north of San Anselmo. Betsy was okay, but she always looked a bit "disheveled" from what I recall. And with all due respect to Reid, Betsy wouldn't have won any beauty contests either. As I remember, Betsy had, what I would charitably call, a bit of a complexion problem.

My mother was really down on Penny, because she lived with her mom on a houseboat in Kentfield. And the locale where those houseboats sat, had a kind of negative connotation, I'm not sure why.

For me, however, Penny was just great. She was extremely good-looking with a nice personality to boot. I recall that she joined us on one of those infamous trips to Vallejo which I earlier discussed. I was sleepy on the way back from Vallejo and I got to put my head on her lap. That was my first real sexual experience, although I didn't even realize it at the time. All I knew then was that I totally enjoyed her lap.

Later in years I would gain more of an appreciation for my mom's disdain of Reid's girlfriends, as I chose my own girlfriends, of which there were few, but with some of those girlfriends more memorable than others.

Perhaps the first was a female student at MCHS, who I'll call "Amanda." She was only about five feet tall and real cute.

As background, MCHS was co-educational; however, the girls and boys were segregated in terms of classes, lunches and other activities with a couple of exceptions, one of which was extracurricular activities such as Dramatic Arts. I participated in a couple of plays in that context: one was called, "The Lottery," and the other was a version of "Our Town."

The Lottery was actually one of three plays, the other two being "Sorry, Wrong Number," and "Egad, What a Gad." Each play involved a competition in the selection of its characters and its director. In turn, there were awards for the best actor, best actress and director, among the three plays.

As to The Lottery, I was competing for one of the main characters named Delacroix. I should mention that the play is very dark and tragic with a public stoning taking place in a village once every year with no one questioning the ritual, just blindly participating in it. In all honesty, I may not have fully grasped the symbolism which is deeply rooted in the play. Like the character Delacroix, I just blindly participated. What irony.

Our director was a student named "John," who happened to be one of the two brightest students in our class. I have to say he did a fantastic job of directing our play. That was validated when he won the best director competition. And he was nice enough to autograph my senior yearbook, saying, "Craig, thanks for being with us in Dramatic Arts, face it, you were great!"

As an aside, the other half of the "two brightest students," was one named "Rod," who graciously inscribed the same yearbook with, "Craig, I don't know where I would be without you in Physics (lab). Thanks a lot for all your help ..."

I have to say, Rod would have been just fine without me, since he seemed to do most of the "heavy lifting" during our lab experiments. He was also a kind and gracious student who I was lucky enough to have as a lab partner.

With respect to The Lottery itself, there were two other students - I'll call "Tall Guy" and "Big Guy" - that I was competing with for the part. They were both much larger than I, Big Guy weighed in at about 250 pounds and played varsity football, and Tall Guy was six foot five and played center on the varsity basketball team. And I was five foot nine and 140 pounds dripping wet. At the outset they made it clear that if I were to "steal" the part away from them (a bit of a Trumpism), they would both beat me up. Hopefully, they were not serious.

Again, long story short, I managed to win that particular competition as I became Delacroix.

Now here's where my memory gets a little fuzzy, so to speak. I do not readily recall the particular play in which I met Amanda. I know that I did meet her in the junior year. So, it must have been in Our Town since The Lottery occurred in our senior year unlike Our Town which took place in our junior year.

In any case, I really grew to like Amanda very much and eventually screwed up enough courage to ask her out. And we ended up dating for quite a while, almost the entire school year (Or did it just seem like that?). However, at some point, we quit dating and for the life of me I can't remember what caused the breakup.

Anyway, that was the absolute best period for me in high school. We did many things together including going out once or twice every weekend and taking trips up the coast since I had a car and a driver's license.

And her father was the manager of a local theater where Amanda worked part time. So, on Friday nights she'd get me in for free to watch whatever movie was playing while she took tickets, which was a nice byproduct of the relationship.

In any event, when Amanda and I first dated we tended to stay out quite late. The first time that happened was on a Friday night when I didn't get home until three in the morning. Apparently my mother was aware of that since the next day she lectured me on the subject, telling me that was much too late to be out. Unfortunately, she didn't tell me exactly when I should be home. But I agreed not to stay out that late and said it would never happen again.

We had a date the next night, and so this time I thought I would begin a trial and error approach, and made a point of coming home earlier, this time at 2 am.

So much for trial and error; this was not the time my mother had in mind since I got another lecture the next morning, and quite a stern one at that. And it was kind of downhill ever after that. While she did not say it, I think she wasn't very fond of Amanda who she never actually met. If she had, I think she would have liked her because everybody seemed to like Amanda after meeting her. But I didn't want to chance a potentially volatile meeting between Amanda and mom after those two experiences.

Still not having clear direction on "the lateness" of my dates, I tried to toe the line and get home by midnight on weekends. That seemed to work. Or maybe my mother was getting tired of lecturing and threw in the towel after that.

To be clear, there was nothing untoward, promiscuous may be a more accurate term, going on between Amanda and myself. My mom may just have been thinking "worst case" all that time she was watching the clock and worrying about her younger son. That's a kind way of saying she wasn't quite ready to be a grandmother.

I will briefly skip forward from the high school years to a time when I was in college for another example of how my parents reacted to my girlfriends, with Sally as the example this time.

Sally's parents owned a cabin in Mendocino, and they had no problem whatsoever allowing us to go there for an overnight stay. As I mentioned earlier, they were fairly liberal and open-minded about most things.

On one of these occasions, Sally and I stopped by my parents' house in Santa Venetia for dinner and an overnight stay prior to continuing on up north. I'm not quite sure what mom and dad had in mind relative to our sleeping arrangements that evening since they only had one spare bedroom in the small house. However, I learned as the night proceeded that we did not have to concern ourselves about that aspect. And it wasn't good.

When we were together, Sally and I would often engage in debating a wide range of subjects. She always took the liberal stance while I was the conservative and this particular evening was no different as we also engaged with my parents on a subject that I no longer can remember. I don't think it was that controversial except that at some point it got a little heated with Sally actually defending my stance on an issue.

I recall that I had had a very bad work day that day and Sally knew it. Otherwise she probably would have let things go, but knowing how bad I felt she was defending me to the point where she actually offended my mother.

This was a point wherein my father decided he needed to step in and defend his partner as well. And step in he did. Not only did he raise his voice to both of us, but he also went and got our two suitcases and before we knew it, had thrown both of them out on the front porch.

He was probably so angered by then, he didn't realize the consequences of what he had done. Sally and I both had a considerable amount of alcohol at that point, and that meant we were looking toward a one hundred forty mile drive late at night on roads I wasn't particularly familiar with.

I don't know how I managed to pull it off, but I drove those one hundred forty miles in a drunken haze and eventually got us to the Mendocino cabin in one piece, no thanks to my dad. Although I love my parents and have forgiven them for their actions at that time, I will never forget their behavior. It didn't matter who was right or who was wrong, you don't throw two drunks out to drive in that condition. Especially when they're your flesh and blood.

I've always wondered if they were ever sorry for that.

In any case, this is yet another example of how my parents treated a girlfriend of mine. Sally never again met with my parents after that night. And I don't know if my parents would have ever overlooked that incident if Sally and I had married.

More than likely, I have to say, we would have been in deep do-do as was the case with my brother and Gina at that time. And I'm almost ashamed to say that I ended up taking my parents' side in their "family feud" with Reid and Gina.

I say "almost ashamed," because with hind sight I understand the situation better than I did at the time. I should not have taken sides; however, it was to a degree understandable since I was around my parents more than I was my brother. At the time I was probably fearful of how my parents would react if I continued to see my brother.

This situation was finally corrected decades into the future when my brother and I had a great reunion.

More on that later.

10 - Reid to the Rescue

Granted, my parents had a feud with Reid and his wife, Gina, a feud that I unfortunately got sucked into. While it may have been understandable given my proximity to my parents, it wasn't right. So, to remedy that situation, I'll take a moment and pay a kind of tribute to a brother who was there when I needed him.

I'll do that by highlighting a situation that occurred during my high school years. It was at a time that I wasn't yet driving, and I routinely hitchhiked home almost every day, going straight home if I lucked out. Other times it turned into a two-stage hitch-hike process, from Kentfield to San Rafael, and then from San Rafael to my home in Santa Venetia.

It was on one of those two-stage days that I was standing on a corner in San Rafael when three older guys saw me and didn't like the fact that I was competing with them for a ride. No sooner than I saw them, they approached me and told me to get out of their area. I was stupid and told them I would do no such thing, upon which one of these brash thugs hauled off and hit me in the chin. Ouch!

I got the message and moved down the street a couple of blocks further. Ironically, I still managed to get a ride before them. The gentleman saw my chin and asked if I was okay. I said, "Sure, I'm fine, thanks for asking."

But I clearly wasn't fine when I got home and relayed the story to my mom. No sooner than I finished telling her, my brother arrived home from work, whereupon I repeated a more abridged version to him.

He told me to get in his car and we'd take a quick ride to San Rafael. I wasn't sure what Reid had in mind when I said, "What are we doing?" He replied something like, "We're going to correct this situation, okay?" To which I replied, "But there were three of them!"

Correct it we did as he raced down the street and drove up onto a curb where the three thugs were still trying to hail a ride. Reid vaulted out of the car, ran toward them, and then jumped on top of one of them, pummeling him into the ground as the other two looked aghast. That was all the time Reid needed to jump on one of those guys who had wisely decided he should flee the scene lest he also get pummeled.

Of course at this point the whole affair began to attract a sizeable crowd and the crowd attracted a traffic cop who was on foot nearby. He approached Reid and the bloodied ruffians, attempting to separate them without much success. Reid decided at that stage that he got the message across and stepped aside less he might end up in jail himself.

The cop began to interrogate, and he started with me.

I explained what had happened earlier and he apparently believed me since my chin was still bloodied. He looked at the two goons who were still on the scene, looked at my brother and me, and then said to me, "Would you like to press charges?" I looked at the two for a bit, then said something like, "No, I think the situation has already been corrected, officer."

He then took the others aside and gave them some kind of a lecture.

Our mission was completed. And from that day on I looked at my brother from a totally different perspective.

11 - Life on Greenfield

After the "bulkhead" experience, my parents considered buying another home but eventually decided that renting one was the way to go. That's where "Greenfield" came into play.

The street was at an interesting locale, in San Anselmo, but bordering San Rafael. So, I could be in San Anselmo one moment, and after just a few steps be in San Rafael the next.

We lived at that address for the remaining time I was attending St. Anselm's School. I remember one day when my friend, Michael, suggested we ride our bikes to school as opposed to having our parents take us. After a bit of "negotiation," my mom finally caved in and agreed to that mode of getting to school.

Beyond that experience, I'm unable to recall anything particularly notable about my life on this border-line street called Greenfield Avenue.

Oh, wait, maybe one or two exceptions. There was a girl that lived next to Michael that I really liked. Her name was Vicky, ironically the same name as another girl I would become quite enamored with almost a decade later. So I used any excuse I could to visit my friend, Michael, who lived up the lane alongside our house. And most of the time Vicky would be outside doing whatever kids that age, I think about twelve or thirteen at that time, do.

It was a harmless relationship that really never ever got off the ground. I think I was a little frustrated that things didn't progress more than they did.

What was more interesting about this particular period in time were the cars that my brother bought as he turned sixteen years old, got his first driver's license and became a real "car guy." And, as it turned out, he turned those cars over as often as I did cats.

I remember the first one was a 1940 Ford, which was a really neat metallic blue in color. Beyond the blue color, however, there was not anything particularly special about that automobile.

Again, being the car guy he was, shortly thereafter he "traded up" to a 1947 Ford he bought from our uncle's wife, Marian. What was especially interesting about this car was that he and I spray-painted two white stripes on it extending from the hood, over the top and down through the trunk.

Since the rest of the car was black as asphalt, it literally looked like a two-lane road. And it did get a lot of "looks" whenever he drove it.

But he didn't have that '47 Ford for very long when he eyed another vehicle that he wanted. This one was a two-tone black and white 1954 Chevy. And it was a bit more in tune with the times. I think that car was my favorite.

Well, while at Greenfield, he made his final purchase, this time a brand spanking new 1960 Pontiac Catalina, bronze in color. The Pontiac had a manual transmission which Reid converted from a shifter on the steering wheel to one on the floor. That was neat. Also the car had what was called "Tri-Power." That referred to three two-barrel carburetors on the engine, with that engine developing 318 horsepower, which was a lot at that time. Fuel injection had not yet arrived on the scene.

Reid actually wanted a model with a more advanced camshaft and thirty extra horsepower.

Because of Reid's age, however, my father took him to the Pontiac dealership, Bianco Motors in San Rafael, to buy the car from a guy named "Chip" who my father knew. Reid really wanted that 348 hp model, but our dad said that 318 should be plenty of horse power to get Reid to where he needed to go. Which was getting to high school and his job at the Mill Valley Purity Store where he worked part time.

What was cool about all of this was when I turned sixteen, Reid let me drive his car on weekends when he wasn't home and didn't need it. (He went hunting a lot. More on that in the next episode.) That's probably when I first learned to drive a manual transmission vehicle. And with that experience, from there on out most of my car purchases were of the manual variety.

What I really liked to do with Reid's Pontiac (when he wasn't around, of course) was to take the air filter off the carburetors which resulted in a "throatier" sound as I accelerated quickly causing even more "throatiness." I particularly recall one day when I tried this tactic, accelerating down a nearby street in Santa Venetia only to have Chip (who I found out unfortunately lived on that particular street) flag me down, thus ruining my fun. He also gave me a lecture about driving fast in residential areas.

There was an exception or two to my driving cars with that form of transmission beginning when I turned sixteen and my mom was good enough to gift me with her 1956 Pontiac and its automatic transmission.

I "modified" that car by changing out the existing hub caps with little knobby ones which I thought looked really cool. No stripes down the middle or anything else of a radical nature. Just the knobby hubs.

And almost overnight I became a very popular student at Marin Catholic High School because now I could take my friends (as well as some students I barely knew!) to all sorts of places such as basketball games and other school-related activities.

I recall one night particularly, in a fierce rainfall, I drove six of us to a basketball game in Santa Clara. My passengers may not have realized it, but I was scared sh**t-less driving in those conditions. Somehow we managed to get to that game and back in one piece.

That used 1956 Pontiac would serve me well until my first purchase, which was a used sky blue 1962 Pontiac Catalina. I think I bought it from the same place that Reid bought his '60 Pontiac.

With respect to the cars my dad bought, he did tend to go in streaks, and they were always General Motors (GM) built cars. His first streak was actually a 1949 Buick (I don't remember the specific model), followed by a 1955 Buick for him and my mom after she gave me her Pontiac. Then there were the Pontiacs, starting with the 1956 one. Although that one really didn't qualify as a streak as the next one was a used Caddy which I think was a 1965 model. And then he progressed to a very large finned 1968 Cadillac, also used. And that may have been the last car in his life that my dad bought.

I did learn a valuable lesson from my dad regarding automobiles; always buy an auto which is two or three years old. There's enough depreciation at that point resulting in savings to the buyer, but not so much as to affect the quality of the car.

And there are other memories of life on Greenfield. There was one which really stands out for me. I had given my mom a nice red GE clock radio for her birthday. I even remember it cost me $44 at the time. There was a minor scratch on it at the Macy's store where I bought it. This was probably my first instance of "negotiating" on the purchase of an item. I called the scratch to the attention of the sales person, and asked if they had another one without scratches. When he said, unfortunately, that this was the last one they had, I told him I'd buy it but I wanted a discount. So, the $49.95 price tag was dropped to the $44.95 that I ultimately paid, and I walked out of the store convinced I was a pretty savvy customer. Particularly for a twelve year old.

And this trait would continue to serve me well in the future, especially when I negotiated the purchase of a new car. I've walked out of more than one showroom when the dealer wouldn't meet my price. And each time that salesperson would come after me.

But back to the clock radio. Sometimes in the afternoon, when there was nothing else to do, I would sit with my mom in the living room watching stuff on TV. On one particular afternoon, the clock radio in her bedroom had been mistakenly set for 5:30 pm (rather than 5:30 am). The volume had been set at the loudest possible setting, don't ask me why. It wasn't even set at a particular radio station.

So, here we are sitting and enjoying TV, when out of the blue something sounding like a freight train running through the house was emitted from the radio. In a flash my mother and I jumped up from our respective chairs and went running for the door to escape whatever awful thing was headed our way. And here's the really funny part. As we approached the front door, each of us was pushing the other to get out that door fast to save our skins from whatever was coming. I'm pushing mom and she's pushing me.

Once we're outside, we calm down and think this thing through, realizing it was just the radio.

So, I apologized to my mom for pushing her. Then I asked her why she was pushing me. To which she responds, "Oh, dear, I wasn't pushing you out of the way. I was really trying to clear the way so you could get out first."

Right, Mom.

12 - Oh, A Hunting We Will Go!

One other Greenfield memory. I mentioned that my brother went hunting a lot with his friends. One was named "Barry," a big hulking Swede who loved to lift weights.

I think my mom was giving my brother a bad time for not taking me on his hunting trips. That was probably the kind of thing that eventually caused a rift between my parents and Reid. I shouldn't have whined about it in the first place. (I admit I whined a lot about stuff like that, and I shouldn't have.)

So, he finally relents. Not only does he take me on his next hunting trip, but he also buys me a really nice Winchester lever action rifle. Off we go, with Barry the Swede as well, up north to an area where they often went to do hunting stuff, like shooting poor innocent deer.

Despite my wanting to go on a hunting trip, I wasn't really into this shooting dear stuff. So, when I had an opportunity to shoot one myself, Reid encouraged me by saying, "Take your shot, Craig," at which point I purposely shot way over the dear's head. It then vanishes into the brush.

Reid and Barry could tell I wasn't just a lousy shot; I had deliberately overshot that poor creature.

And here's the funny part, although it wasn't funny at the time. I learned that a big part of the whole hunting ritual was sitting around the campfire at night, drinking and telling stories. So, there we were, me, Reid and Big Swede, doing that campfire stuff (although I didn't get to drink anything alcoholic). In the process, they began chiding me for my earlier performance or lack of same, then telling me I would be given a thirty second head start, after which they would come after me. It wasn't clear to me what they would do if they found me, however.

I didn't need any more encouragement; I took off into the darkened woods, running as fast as I could, at one point falling flat on my face. I can hear them shouting as they drew closer to me, "Hey Craig, we're gonna get you!" Then they shoot their rifles in the air a few times for effect.

My heart races as I continue to retreat. And then the gun fires stop and there is absolute quiet in those woods. After a while, not knowing what else to do, I sheepishly return to the campfire, which I still could see from the distance.

And that's when the two of them jumped out from behind a tree, shouting "Boo!" At which point I think I peed in my pants.

After that adventure, I never whined about not going hunting ever again.

However, there was one other time I went hunting with Reid.

That time it was just the two of us, I recall. On this particular occasion, Reid and I were covering a lot of ground. I certainly had no idea of the direction we were going in or where we were in relation to where we had started from. We had no compass or any other device to assist us in our adventure.

Ultimately, we got to a point where we had given up the hunt, so to speak. No deer or anything else for me not to shoot at. We agreed to return to the campsite. But where was that?

While neither of us would admit it, we were lost. No doubt about it. I don't know about Reid, but I was almost in panic mode. Soon it would be dark, and then we'd really be in trouble.

Low and behold, we spotted what looked like a road down beneath us. If it was a road we could just follow it until we got somewhere we recognized and then be able to return to our campsite. So, down we went to "the road."

Until we got a bit closer, that was, and we realized what we thought was a road, due to its paved appearance, was actually a very large boulder!

I was beside myself. What were we going to do?

Well, I'm still here, aren't I? So, there had to be a happy ending to this story, as Reid slowly and methodically managed to find us our way back to camp.

That was the last time I went hunting.

One last Greenfield memory. It was at the start of the 1960s, and we would shortly move to Santa Venetia when my dad entered into the partnership in buying the supermarket there.

The prior decade, the 1950s, was an odd period. And there were some negative aspects, primary among them the Cold War between Russia and our country.

And there was a rumor circulating that the Pope opened a letter written a long time ago. It had something to do with civilization and what would happen next. In any case, as the story goes, when the Pontiff opened and read the mysterious letter, he fainted.

At least that was the rumor circulating. I think it was a St. Anselm's School rumor at that.

With the oncoming 1960s, however, there was hope and a more positive vibe. Particularly among Roman Catholics who witnessed the election of a Catholic president, John F. Kennedy. That had been a major issue during that election.

Kennedy was interesting in terms of the relationship between his religion and his politics. Like President Eisenhower before him, Kennedy attended church services regularly, and used religious rhetoric in his speeches; however, unlike Eisenhower he maintained a much stricter separation between church and state. And, although relatively unknown at the time, beneath his commanding public persona there were private vices that contradicted his faith. One such example is an alleged relationship he had with the actress Marilyn Monroe.

Unfortunately, our 35th president, John F. Kennedy, was assassinated on Friday, November 22, 1963, in Dallas, Texas.

Second Piece: The College Years

1 - The College Experience

It's almost cliché to say, but I will anyway; I was the first in my family to go to college. My parents didn't go there. Brother Reid didn't go either. He became a plumber, probably making more money than I ever would, even with my college education and, eventually, two graduate degrees.

And I might not have gone to college if it weren't for the fact that most of my classmates at Marin Catholic High School were talking about going.

My parents never even said that I should move on to post-secondary education. It was all my idea. But I really didn't have a clue about where I should look for the "college experience." So I ordered a book I think was put out by the folks who do the "SAT" (Standard Aptitude Test); I don't know their name off the top of my head.

So, armed with that book, I began my search. No sooner than I started that, I realized that I would need to take those SAT tests for places I would apply to. That was an experience in itself.

There was something called the "PSAT" which was a kind of test to get you familiar with what the SAT itself would be like. I don't recall how I performed on that particular exam. However, some things stick with you throughout your life; such was the case with my test scores on the actual SAT exams.

You could take the exams more than once. So, the first one I took offered up a score of 1137 out of a possible 1600. That's about 71% which you'd think was not such a great performance; however, those percentages are deceiving since I learned that such a score put me in a percentile higher than that percentage.

After taking the SAT the first time, I was surprised, and quite pleased, when the high school principal, Father Dullea, intercepted me at recess and told me that that was a good score, but I could do even better by buying a book which had SAT-like problem/questions and studied it. So, I did that.

It paid off handsomely as I managed to score just over 1200 on the next round.

I was ecstatic, particularly when I learned that that score qualified me for a California State Scholarship. Fortunately for my dad, but unfortunately for me, my dad was doing pretty well, salary-wise, at the time (with the Santa Venetia Supermarket) and that likely precluded me from qualifying for an actual scholarship since it was also "need-based."

That was a little bit of a disappointment, but I was still pleased, particularly since at graduation it was announced that I was a qualifier for that scholarship based on my SAT scores. I don't recall how many students were in that illustrious group;

I think it was about thirty-something out of a class of 150 students. But my score actually paled in comparison to two of the brighter students in our class, my director-friend, John, and my lab partner, Rod, who achieved scores approaching the 1400 level. And there were actually some bright students somewhere in the country scoring a perfect 1600. Amazing!

Now back to the college experience itself. After reviewing the section of the book which I earlier referred to, that provided descriptions of hundreds of colleges, I decided to apply to three universities, all of which were Jesuit schools: University of San Francisco (USF), Santa Clara University (SCU) and Seattle University (SU).

Other than the fact that they were Jesuit colleges, there was no particular reason why I chose these three; however, two of them were relatively local and the third was out of the area and might be an interesting experience.

I was accepted at USF and Seattle University, but not at Santa Clara. I think the reason I wasn't accepted at the latter was the fact that the USF program in engineering that I applied for involved three years at USF and then a transfer to Santa Clara for the last two years. Since I had acknowledged that in my applications, Santa Clara probably gave other students greater consideration. At least, that was my rationalization at the time.

So I needed to choose between a school in the northwest, or the more local USF.

Now I had a good high school friend, I'll call this character "Ron", who also applied and was accepted to USF. He would be in pre-med. He encouraged me to go to USF where we could both be roommates in a dormitory. Trying to convince me of that, he told me that I wouldn't like Seattle with all its rain.

I probably shouldn't have listened to good friend Ron. As it turned out, his mother told him (if he was telling the truth) that he should room with someone who would also be pre-med. So much for the roommate experience, which I will come back to later. (Actually, USF was probably a better choice for me for more than one reason.)

So, here I was headed to USF for that "college experience" I was looking forward to. But, once I got there I found my pre-engineering coursework to be quite challenging as I struggled to maintain a 2.0 GPA for the first two semesters. That was until I began to work much harder at my studies the following two semesters, and as a result, was rewarded with a 3.0 GPA.

However, I began to have "delusions of grandeur" thinking that with my improved grades maybe I should consider a transfer to one of the campuses of the prestigious University of California (UC).

That's where things got messy. I initially applied to UC Santa Barbara (UCSB) and was accepted there. I would have been in their mechanical engineering program. However, somewhere along the way, my interests shifted from engineering to architecture. I think that arose from a movie I saw about an architect, played by Kirk Douglas, but I don't recall the name of that movie.

So, before I even got to UCSB, I decided to switch my application to UC Berkeley (Cal) which had an outstanding architectural program. Low and behold that worked as I was accepted into the UC Berkeley program. That was great!

As I will note later on in my story, during the summer of 1966 (before going on to Berkeley) I met a girl named Vicky who I really liked and was starting at UCSB in the fall. I could have kicked myself for switching my application to Cal!

Long story short, things did not go well for me at Cal the first two quarters. I began to see an unfortunate pattern here after my prior poor experience the first two semesters at USF. However, this time around there was ample justification arising from a bad case of mononucleosis and a severe depression over Vicky's departure and my GPA showed it, plummeting below a 2.0, as I suddenly found myself "out on the college street."

Now, it didn't have to be that way since the university had offered me some options after the first quarter: I could drop out for a quarter until my health improved, or I could take advantage of an on-campus parking spot so I wouldn't have to walk to the campus from my dormitory.

While I took advantage of the campus parking slot, with hindsight I should have taken the first option and dropped out until my health improved.

As I said earlier, some things stick with you throughout life and such was my experience with a particular math course, Math 111, treating the subject of linear algebra (It's all about matrices, eigenvalues and eigenvectors). This was a difficult subject area. In addition to my mononucleosis, I was taking a difficult course taught by an instructor who wasn't particularly fluent in the English language and a textbook that apparently had been translated from its original Russian version and not very well at that.

And as if that weren't enough, I was under the impression that I was taking Math 111 as a "pass/fail," which meant that there was no grade to impact my GPA if things went south.

Well, things did go south when I was notified halfway through the semester that it could not be taken pass/fail since it was a required course (or curse?) in my program.

I recall asking the professor after I had taken the final exam and knew I hadn't performed well, if "he gave F's." He gave me the most odd look that I can't begin to describe.

I eventually found out that he did, in fact, give F's, which was the outcome of that course experience. And as a result, "my goose was cooked" GPA-wise.

There was a happy ending as it turned out, when a good friend who I'll call "Ted" explained how I could get back into the University. He told me that one of his fraternity colleagues had been in a similar situation. He had flunked out of the University but learned that the School of Agriculture, which had enrollment problems, had a history of "taking in" students in those circumstances. So, upon application he was admitted to the School.

Ted suggested I consider that approach which I did. I had a meeting with a dean of the school during which he inquired as to my seriousness in wanting to go into the field of agriculture, given that I did not have any kind of background in that field. He was well aware of the fact that students oftentimes tried this ruse, with the School getting burned more than once. They'd get admitted, stay for a quarter or two, then transfer out to another school at Cal. I was ready for this and told him about my cousin's sheep ranch, including my interest in such an enterprise. My cousin Claire's husband, Bill Foerstler, a graduate of Cal Davis, really did have a sheep ranch in Petaluma, but it was a stretch to say I had any interest in that area.

I digress. I just noted that my cousin Claire's son, Stephen, was "connected" to me via the Web site 23&me.com. He would be my first cousin, once removed. I have sent Stephen a request to connect back to me and look forward to hearing from him via the Web site. How exciting!

Now, returning to the strategy of going through the School of Agriculture, it worked. I was accepted back into the fold, and eventually wound my way through multiple majors, including agriculture, psychology, and finally business where I ran up a GPA approaching 4.0.

I would graduate after the fall quarter of 1968. But that was not the end of my college experience. I wanted to go to grad school in business. Foolishly, I didn't apply to the prestigious Berkeley program, thinking I wouldn't get in if I did (Dear Reader, never do that!). So, I applied to several schools, including UCLA, where I was ultimately accepted.

I'll save that experience for the next episode in my life.

2 - There's a "Draft" at UCLA

Yes, there was a draft at UCLA, but it had nothing to do with a current of air. It had all to do with conscription into the military.

I had a hard time settling in at UCLA after I was admitted to its graduate level management program. It actually involved leaving the first quarter when I couldn't find adequate housing. That's a story in itself.

I waited until I got down to LA to find a place to live on or off campus. I saw a place advertised in Venice and I thought it would be neat to live on the beach, but once I got there I found that Venice, at least at that time, was not such a great place to live. So I aborted the effort, gave up and went back home to Santa Venetia.

From home I was able to identify an on-campus dormitory for graduate students. I returned to UCLA the next quarter and settled into my new dorm home. It didn't amount to much, not even a TV. So off I went driving around at night looking for a store selling small TVs until I was able to find and buy one.

That drive all over town at night did nothing for my morale. It went beyond a morale problem; I was utterly and totally depressed. More than once I longed for my Bay Area home and Sally, who I left behind.

As it turned out this was not an auspicious time to be going to grad school. The country was engaged in a war in Viet Nam, a war it had no business being in, in the first place. To top that off, there was a process of conscription, referred to as "the draft."

On December 1, 1969, something called the Selective Service System conducted two lotteries to determine the order-of-call to military service in the Viet Nam War for men born from January 1, 1944, to December 31, 1950. My November 2, 1946, birthdate qualified me for inclusion in that group.

Reinstitution of the lottery was a change from the system of drafting the oldest men first, which was formerly the determining method for order of call.

There were 366 capsules containing birth dates placed in a large glass container and drawn by hand to assign order-of-call numbers to all men within the 18 to 26 age range specified in the Selective Service law. A separate drawing was held to determine order-of-call for men with the same date.

I recall watching the process unfold on TV as some guy reached into the container and pulled out a date. I don't recall what that first date was, but whoever was unlucky enough to be born on that particular date was headed for the military, as that date was assigned the number one.

The drawing continued until all days of the year were assigned numbers.

Although I didn't, I could have stopped watching the process when those born on November 2nd, my birthdate, were assigned number 34. It was a done deal that I would be called up very soon. They were going to take the first 30 in January and then continue on each month thereafter.

My reluctance to enter the military had nothing to do with a lack of patriotism on my part; however, I didn't want to be involved in this war, a war many would label "unjust." I wanted to finish grad school and then, at some future date, I'd apply to an Officer Candidate School with the U. S. Navy and do my service. Hopefully, not in Viet Nam.

But that wasn't going to happen given number 34.

I sat there, transfixed by the unfolding process.

The day after the numbers were drawn, I decided to go to the campus library to review my options in terms of deferments to see if there was some physical or mental reason that I could be excused from service.

I recall that time like it was only yesterday. It was absolutely beautiful walking across the campus that day. And the "draft gods" were looking favorably at me when I ran across someone I knew from the dorm who was a dentistry student. He asked me why I seemed to be in such a rush, so I explained my predicament to him.

He then asked me to open my mouth and say "ahh" which I did. Whereupon he commented, "Your teeth need some serious correction. You should see an orthodontist."

My reply at the time, "Alright, but that's the least of my worries right now. I need to handle this draft situation first."

And then he replied, "Take care of your orthodontics and you wouldn't need to be concerned about the draft. The military doesn't want to have to deal with your orthodontics."

I couldn't believe it and asked him to explain further. Yes, there were provisions for physical deferments and one of them addressed things like orthodontics. I even went to the library to verify what he said.

He was right.

After the trip to the UCLA library, I continued to mull over my options. Do I accept my fate and await induction? Or do I look for a way to avoid being inducted?

The next day I made my decision. I wasn't going to accept my fate. At that point I knew what I needed to do.

I didn't even go to classes. What would be the point of that?

So I packed up my belongings, got in my car and headed for home, this time to find a cooperative orthodontist. I believe I tried to explain to my parents what I was going to do. I honestly don't recall what their reaction was at the time. I do know that my father didn't share my disgust for the War.

After that, I went about the process of finding an orthodontist. I don't recall his name, but that doesn't really matter. He practiced in San Rafael, not far from home.

I don't know what his position was on the War; I was honest and explained to him my rationale for having orthodontics performed on my teeth. And I would need a letter from him, explaining why I was having orthodontics. He was also honest and said he could accommodate that as long as I cooperated, that meaning my showing up for appointments once I presented that letter to the draft board.

I easily agreed to that.

3 - Back to the Blue and Gold

I still wanted to continue my graduate education, but it couldn't be at UCLA. So, I did something that I should have done all along, I applied to my alma mater's prestigious Graduate School of Business (now the Haas School of Business) at UC Berkeley. I really didn't think I'd get in, but it was worth a try, I thought.

And did I get surprised! I was accepted for the upcoming quarter.

Once again, life was worth living, not having to worry about a trip to Viet Nam. So, for the next six quarters straight, I attended classes at Berkeley, commuting from home as opposed to living near campus. That saved some money as my parents and I divvied up the grad school costs.

And, once again, I'll "toot my own horn" regarding my performance during those six quarters.

There were twelve courses in my MBA program, all at the graduate level except for two. The coursework included, but was not limited to, the following subjects: quantitative decision-making, business economics, regional economics, organizational behavior, business research and economic forecasting, as well as four independent research courses.

How did I do? All "A's," with one exception, a "B" in the organizational behavior course. Not sure what happened there since I got a straight "A" in org behavior years later in a doctoral level course. Se la vie.

In any case, that performance yielded a nifty 3.84 GPA for the MBA program.

Those six quarters were trying in more than one way, however. I had lived either on, or near, campus during my undergraduate years. At USF I had lived in Phelan Hall on the university campus. First, in one room during my freshman year and then another room in what was called "the annex" to Phelan Hall, the second year. (I will discuss my college roommates at Phelan Hall in a future episode).

My living arrangements as an undergraduate at Berkeley were a bit more "erratic" than when I was at USF.

Once I arrived on campus in 1966, I proceeded to occupy a succession of living quarters. First, a dormitory that only housed upper division and graduate students. It was called "Mitchell-Peixoto" (pronounced "Pishoto") Hall. Quite an experience which, again, I'll discuss a bit later.

Subsequently, I had three abodes, living in a rooming house on Durant Avenue one quarter, an apartment on College Avenue for the summer quarter, and then to a large three bedroom apartment, shared with two others, on Arch Street north of campus for the duration of my college life.

The point I'm trying to make is that as an undergraduate I did not live at home and commute (which I could have done, but didn't) to Berkeley. This changed dramatically when I started the graduate program during which time I lived at home and commuted to campus every day I attended classes.

I did this for more than one reason, the main one being cost considerations. Since my parents paid my full fare for the undergraduate years, I wasn't inclined to ask them to do the same for my graduate studies. I worked part-time and they did help a bit with some of my tuition expense.

I found that living at home while pursuing studies at the University had its own disadvantages, nonetheless. And a good example of that was during the period of time that students and non-students alike were confronting campus police over the issue of People's Park."

The Park was a vacant lot near campus and some folks thought it should not be occupied by anyone other than those folks themselves. It was a complex issue that can't be easily treated in a few words, so I won't even try to do that.

The important point herein is that the confrontations with police became so volatile that one day the police "tear-gassed" a crowd of students near Sproul Hall, the administration building, to get them to disburse. (Note that by 2021, the park was still sitting there as the Regents planned to build dorms on the site. Good luck on that!)

Unfortunately, I was leaving campus at that point, and headed to the lot where my car was parked. And little did I know that I would be one of the unsuspecting folks that got caught up in the whole mélange as I innocently proceeded in that direction.

Long story, short, I was gassed along with anyone else in the area, having to retreat to the nearest restroom to try and wash my blinded eyes.

That was bad enough, until I got home and told the story to my parents, at which point my father tells me, "It's your fault, you shouldn't have been there! What were you thinking of!"

I shouldn't have been on the campus where I take classes? I shouldn't have walked across campus to get to my car? Where should I have been?

The whole point of this narrative is that on more than one occasion my father could be just a bit unreasonable, and this was one of those times. And he would repeat that kind of behavior sometime later over something my girlfriend Sally said to my mother.

Now to return to the subject of my graduate studies. In terms of academics, my field of emphasis in the MBA program was applied economics since I enjoyed that subject field as an undergraduate. And for my master's thesis, a pretty nice guy named Leonard Merewitz served as my advisor. He had recently received his Ph. D. in the econ department at Berkeley and provided excellent oversight for my thesis.

I also worked with Dr. Merewitz at the Institute of Business and Economic Research on campus and he included me in several of his writing efforts at the time.

I remember particularly the research I did for his book, "The Budget's New Clothes," (which he co-authored with Stephen Sosnick of UC Davis) a critique of planning-programming-budgeting systems (PPBS), which had been the prevailing approach to Federal budgeting in that era.

As a side observation, in the "Authors' Note" at the end of his book, Merewitz acknowledged that planning-programming-budgeting systems was being abandoned by the Federal government. But he also noted that certain aspects of PPBS would continue, such as multi-year costing.

All the same, he was kind enough to give me credit in his preface to the book (e.g., "Ang Kiat-Poon and Craig Blake were also very helpful") as well as in several other places. My work focused on the use of cost-benefit analysis in such matters as the demand function for recreation.

My other "contribution" relates to my observation that I didn't think the title of his book was appropriate; I thought it was a tad silly, although I didn't quite phrase it like that.

While he did make some changes based on my various observations, it goes without saying that Leonard Merewitz didn't take me up on that particular suggestion. He really liked that title.

During the course of my MBA studies, I held some jobs including a part-time one at a CPA firm in San Rafael. I don't recall how I landed that job.

Although I took some courses, I didn't have an accounting degree so the work at that firm was largely clerical; I particularly remember working on a "bruning" machine which copied the tax forms prepared by the accountants in the firm. Did a lot of bruning, I must admit. But the pay was good and I liked the people there.

Coincidentally, one of those people was a guy named Mike who happened to be married to a girl that I had dated in high school named Julie. She was actually a cousin of Reid's wife Gina. Julie's parents owned the restaurant, San Rafael Joes.

Sally and I double-dated with Mike and Julie and on one of those dates, we went to San Rafael Joes for dinner.

Years later my wife Elena and I would also go to San Rafael Joes.

I must now digress. Reid and Gina had two sons, Scott and Steven, who I hadn't seen in many years. And Scott, the older son, worked part-time at the restaurant. On the night we were there, Scott happened to be working at his bus boy job. He came to our table to clear things up as bus boys do. That's when Elena made a point of telling him I was his "Uncle Craig." And although he wouldn't remember it, I was also his Godfather.

Sixteen year old Scott got a big grin on his face, as we shook hands and exchanged a few pleasantries. It was a bittersweet moment for me and perhaps also for Scott. And I was sad that we hadn't been close in the years since he was first christened.

Years later that would change. I'll discuss it in a little bit.

Getting back to the subject of Mike and Julie. It is noteworthy to mention that Mike and I became friends since he, too, was going through the graduate MBA program at Berkeley. Once we learned that, we agreed to commute together for our classes. That worked out well.

I haven't seen Mike and Julie for a few years. Unfortunately, the last time I did see them was at my brother Reid's funeral at St. Rafael's Church. We've exchanged Christmas cards but that's about it for the years since. And recently I received a card from them explaining that they had bought a home in San Jose.

Maybe I'll see them again one of these days.

4 - Five Years of My Life

As noted elsewhere, when I wasn't awarded the permanent position of assistant superintendent for business services at the Oakland Unified School District, and asked the reason why, I was told the successful applicant had a doctoral degree. That was sufficient grounds for me to go for one more advanced degree, having already completed my MBA at Berkeley.

A bit later in this memoir in five pieces, I will discuss the impact of my doctoral program on my family, especially Elena. Here, however, I'm going to discuss how I selected a suitable program, the program itself and the steps leading up to my ultimate graduation from that program.

My options, in terms of an appropriate program, were few and far between. I needed one that would "work" in my particular situation. The situation? Living in the SF Bay Area and working full time. At that time it was with the Orinda Union School District, a short commute from our home in Pinole.

As I surveyed the field of possible "candidates," I automatically eliminated those of not great distinction. Lest I offend someone who's received their degree from one of those institutions, I will not name them. In the end, I decided that there were two programs that met my needs. One was a doctoral program in management offered by Claremont Graduate University. It was clearly a distinguished program and it addressed the subject area that supported my professional goals. This particular program, of course, was based in Claremont, California.

The second program was one offered by the University of Southern California, and was based in the University's Sacramento Public Affairs Center in Sacramento, California. This program awarded the successful candidate a doctorate in public administration, a degree which would also support my professional needs.

The USC program was not only a distinguished one, but it was also ranked the third best program in the country in that field. I believe the top two were also private schools, both on the east coast, a bit of a "commute" for me.

Neither program was cheap. Both programs entailed about five years of coursework, oral and written exams, both culminating with a doctoral dissertation.

I was leaning toward the Claremont program since it was in management, a bit broader than the very distinguished USC public administration program. However, it entailed long trips to southern California with the accompanying costs for hotels and meals. I concluded that the USC program offered at the Sacramento Public Affairs Center best met my needs.

The application process involved submitting transcripts of all my college courses, both undergraduate and graduate. It also required multiple references (I don't recall exactly how many) and an essay discussing my "World View." That last one stumped me a bit and I had to call someone who administered the program who could more clearly define what "World View" meant in their context.

After completing the application process, all I could do was wait and wonder if I would be accepted by the illustrious institution that is the University of Southern California.

After a few weeks of nervous anticipation, I was notified of my acceptance.

Being accepted is one thing; figuring out how you're going to get through it all is another. It meant at least one trip up to Sacramento for a four day weekend of classwork every month for the next several years, with the accompanying costs of meals and hotels, and the necessary time off from work. Regarding the latter, I had already negotiated with the District the fact that I would be pursuing a degree, and would need to take those days off every month. And I somehow managed to address the cost aspect and its impact on our family budget.

It was now September of 1982, and I was "off to the races." And since I was given considerable credit from my MBA program toward the coursework component, I was able to complete that component in about three years. At that point it became a matter of taking and passing oral and written exams, and completing a dissertation.

There were about eighteen students starting the current year's program. They came from all kinds of backgrounds. Some were not employed at the time. Some were still working like me. And there was even one or two retirees. Several already held an MPA (Master of Public Administration) degree, while a few held other graduate degrees. I think I was the only person with an MBA, if my memory serves me correctly. Most were male but there were some females as well. Ages ranged from twenty-somethings up to one military retiree, who must have been over sixty years old.

I happened to be thirty-five years old at the time and my goal was to complete the program by the time I turned forty. I like having goals.

Throughout the years of coursework for the program, several of us would meet as a "study group" in an effort to better appreciate what we were dealing with, particularly as we approached final exams for those courses. And for the most part I found my colleagues to be interesting folks who were fairly easy to get along with.

By the year 1985, I had completed all required coursework, took and passed oral and written exams, and began working on my dissertation, under the supervision of committee members, John Kirlin, Jeffrey Chapman, and Gary Hoaglander.

The final product, almost 300 pages in length, was entitled, "Budgetary Behavior and Fiscal Outcomes in California School Districts." When I completed the program, I even gave my mother a bound copy of the dissertation for her birthday. I doubt that she read it completely, but she certainly appreciated it since to some degree it reflected her role in getting me to where I was in life. Unfortunately, my father was no longer alive at that point.

Although I completed my degree in the prior December, there were graduation ceremonies the following summer for all those who graduated over the course of the past year.

I had not attended graduation ceremonies for either my bachelor's degree or my MBA degree at UC Berkeley, where you tend to get lost in the crowd of other graduates. However, I decided that I should attend this time around to recognize my achievement as well as to expose my two sons, Matthew and Jeffrey, to what a college graduation was all about since they were still in elementary school.

So, the four of us drove on down to the USC campus (which ironically was the very first time I set foot on that campus) in Los Angeles as I took part in ceremonies for those of us in the public administration program.

I recall that it was a particularly nice summer's day and the campus was absolutely beautiful. I'm glad I finally got to see it.

However, what I am most proud of was the fact that I was only the second person in my class to reach that point. And the guy who graduated just prior to me was retired from the military, had no family, and did not work. Enough said.

I was awarded the DPA degree, Doctor of Public Administration, on December 19, 1986.

5 - College Roommates

Any discussion of college life would be incomplete without discussing the students we lived with during those times.

My first experience with college roommates was when I attended USF, which was only twenty miles from home. I could have commuted to the University but I wanted the "real college experience."

Was I in for a rude awakening on that count.

Originally thinking I would room with a high school friend, who I referred to as "Ron," I ended up having to take whatever was doled out to me when Ron bailed on our "agreement."

So, without my friend Ron as roommate, I was assigned another student who will go unnamed. The reason I won't specify his name is because now I'm going to address a less than positive arrangement. Although some would say it was a great arrangement.

My "roommate" was really not a roommate at all. Why? Well, it had to do with the fact that he lived on the peninsula, Woodside I believe, also not far from campus as was my case.

However, he had a girlfriend who lived relatively close on the peninsula. And as it turned out, he spent his nights living with his girlfriend, not at the dorm, such that his parents didn't know (I assume).

Great for him, not so great for Craig. I effectively had a private room which many students would covet; however, I had planned on having a college experience including a real live roommate. So, it was actually a fairly lonely existence. While other students could have "bull sessions" with their roomies or study together or do whatever other rituals roommates do, I couldn't do those things.

One ritual was going to breakfast, lunch or dinner with your roommate which I obviously couldn't do. So I either went to meals by myself or tried to find some accommodating students at the cafeteria that I could sit with.

I did have some friends from my high school - there were about ten or twelve who went to USF - that I could meet up with, but I really wanted to meet some new folks. My high school friend, Jim, living in a dorm room not that far from mine, was kind enough to include me sometimes when he and his roomie went off to dinner.

So, private room all my freshman year. And I was starting to get used to that almost, but not quite, enjoying my situation.

Well, my sophomore year took care of that. This time around I was assigned a roommate named "Roger." I recall many things about Roger. For example, he was really into our required "military science," otherwise known as ROTC (pronounced

Rot-C) which stands for Reserve Officers Training Corp. He could spit-shine the heck out of those shoes.

Roger was like my previous roommate, in that he too had a girlfriend; however, unlike the first one he didn't go to her place every night since she lived in his native Tucson, Arizona.

He did go home on breaks and longer holidays. Otherwise he was at USF twenty-four hours a day, seven days a week. I recall his first trip home was during our semester break at which time he invited me to visit him, his parents and his girlfriend.

That was quite nice of him.

That stay at his place was interesting to say the least. I particularly remember the night we went to the local drive-in movie. Roger took his girlfriend, of course, and I ended up assigned to his fifteen year old sister. I don't recall her name. However, I was a bit apprehensive since I barely knew the girl. And to make matters even more uncomfortable, she wanted to "neck" in the back seat with me.

Oh, boy! That was really awkward! I didn't know quite what to do with her. After all, she was about five years younger than me, pretty much qualifying me for "robbing the cradle." I'm a little unclear on how things went from there, but I do recall suggesting that I would go get us refreshments. I thought that that would at least get me away from her for a bit. However, she decided that she should accompany me. That was okay; at least we could bring a halt to the necking for a while. And my theory was when we returned to the car,

I could interrupt "the proceedings" as we ate the goodies I bought at the refreshment stand.

I think that at some point she "got the message" about my not wanting to get too close to her. I believe that Roger told me a little later that his sister thought I was too shy and/or I didn't know how to go about necking properly. But it wasn't that and I didn't have the heart to tell Roger that I really wasn't "into" his sister. So I remained "shy Craig." Until the next night when we went to a party somewhere and I met another girl, I don't recall her name, but she was older than Roger's sister at least. I believe she was a senior in high school, which made her only two years younger than I was. I had "graduated" by three years!

And I really liked this girl and was sorry she lived so far away or we could have dated. If my memory serves me right, I believe we actually corresponded with letters for a short period of time. Those were "the olden days" when there was no Internet or email. But I eventually concluded this relationship was going nowhere, and after a time the letters stopped. This girl probably started dating someone else more local anyway. And so, that was that. So much for long-distance romance!

So, those were my two roommates at USF: "Absent Guy" and "ROTC Roger," who I think ended up going all the way with ROTC and into the U. S. Army upon graduation.

Good for Roger! I never followed up with him and I hope he didn't get sent to Viet Nam. But if he did, I sincerely hope that he eventually came home.

He was a good guy.

So, that was it for USF roommates during my two years there. There were more roommates for me when I got to Cal, however, which I will shortly discuss.

Aside from roommates, I did try to maintain a connection with some of my high school classmates who also attended USF.

One of those, named Phil, did not actually live on campus, instead commuting from his parents' home in Kentfield.

Phil was a great guy, and what I would call, a multi-faceted individual, perhaps even a Renaissance Man. At any one time he would be engaged in multiple pursuits. I particularly recall a time when he had completed the fabrication of a canoe, which we took out on the Bay near his home in Kentfield, and then rowed almost to Sausalito and back.

During my sophomore year, Phil also kindly suggested that I join him on the USF yearbook staff. This related to the sports portion of the yearbook for which he was the editor. I was his assistant and even got my name embossed on my own yearbook that year. That was nice.

The year I was his assistant was a rewarding one for the "Dons," the USF basketball team with the likes of Ollie Johnson, Erwin Mueller, Joe Ellis, and Russ Gumina, among others. There was a guard playing on that team, Larry Blum, who was only six feet tall, but could actually dunk the basket because of his jumping skills.

That year the Dons went as far as the regional tournament in Provo, Utah. They beat Oklahoma City in the first round of the playoffs, but then lost to the powerhouse that was UCLA in the second round of tournament play.

In any case, working on the yearbook was an enjoyable diversion from studies that sophomore year. We would write up what happened at the various games, figure out which pictures to use and where to place them, and other related yearbook stuff.

While I'm talking about Phil, I also need to give him credit for organizing a bachelor party for me prior to my wedding with Elena. Joining Phil and me at the Greek Taverna in San Francisco were Jim, Ted and some others I can't seem to recall. I do remember that Phil made a point of giving me some bills (I think they were one dollar bills) to stuff in the waist band of one of the belly dancers.

It was a fun evening.

I didn't participate in sports while I was in college. That doesn't mean that I didn't try out for a team. I actually did, kind of, in a way. That was in my freshman year at USF, when my friend Jim from high school suggested that I run with the cross country team one day. They were going to wind their way from campus through Golden Gate Park and then back to campus. So, he gave me some cleats, which I wasn't at all comfortable wearing, and off I went with Jim and his cross country cohorts that day.

I don't know that I want to discuss how this all played out

since it's a bit embarrassing. But I will anyway. After about, I don't recall, maybe a mile or so, I became very fatigued. So, I found a friendly grove of trees to hide behind, and sat out the rest of the time while the others were running all over hell and tarnation. I was hoping no one would notice, but I'm sure someone must have. Eventually, I returned to the locker room, put the cleats back in Jim's locker, thereby ending my "try out" for the team, as well as "my life in collegiate sports."

As an aside, I need to mention that I brought this incident up with friend Jim via email recently, and he didn't recall it at all. I'm not clear on what he didn't recall, whether it was me joining his team, or me hiding in the bushes.

That's probably just as well.

6 - A Necktie on the Door

Now, back to the discussion of roommates.

When I started at Cal, for my living arrangements, I selected a dormitory up on the hillside that only accepted upper division and graduate students. And, ironically, I got another roommate that was absent a lot. Not every day absent, just absent every few days. He was odd to begin with, a graduate student in mathematics, who would sit on the edge of his bed looking out into space and mumbling something to himself. Probably something mathematical.

When he met this fellow (whose name I can't pull up) my friend Ted commented to me when the roomie was gone, "So how do you like having a Jewish roommate?"

I was caught completely off guard by that remark, saying, "Really? How do you know that?" This reaction reflected my naivete about people as a function of my parochial school existence, which totally excluded Jews and black people, brown people and other minorities for that matter.

Well, as soon as I set foot on the Cal campus, that seeming naivete had been addressed in short order with its tremendous diversity. And, of course, I got a jump start with a Jewish roommate.

I don't recall exactly when it happened, but I shortly put in a request for another room assignment; I hasten to add that it had nothing to do with my roommate being Jewish, although I don't recall exactly what reason I gave.

But with a new room came a new roommate.

His name was Guati (short for Guatimoc) and he hailed from Hermosillo, Mexico, a large city a ways south of the Arizona border in the state of Sonora. We had something in common as he also "fled" his last room in International House, which catered to students from all over the globe. Guati likened that place to "a zoo." Lots of strange folks, he said.

As an aside, I should note that Guati was not only bilingual, but also very personable, and had "dabbled" in politics to varying degrees. I believe he was the student body president for his former University of Sonora. And he might have been the mayor of his home town of Hermosillo (but don't quote me on that).

In any case, I must say that my living environment worked out much better with Guati as roommate; we were not only copasetic with each other, but became very good friends. As a matter of fact, I would include both Guati and Ted in the category of my very best friends at the time.

Unfortunately, Ted himself would be unable to continue in that status a few years down the line for reasons I will revisit a bit later.

Regarding our rooming arrangements, however, Guati and I soon agreed that the dorm we were in was not to our liking. So, we started to look around for another place to hang our hats and eventually found it in a rooming house on Durant Street, only a two block walk from campus.

There was only one other resident in the place, a graduate math student named Javier. And he was quite a character. But the rooming house itself was run by a very old lady named Mrs. Loggie, who was hard of hearing.

And that is quite a story in itself.

Mrs. Loggie didn't suffer fools gladly and she had very strict rules, including no girls in the all-male establishment. Since my friend and roommate Guati was quite the lady's man, we would soon learn that our lives in the rooming house were destined for failure.

Although the bedroom was quite large, we did have to share it so Guati had this interesting strategy of putting a necktie on the outside door handle of our room when he had female company. So, when I returned from the library or somewhere else on campus, I would know that he had female company and didn't want his activity interrupted, in which case I would go downstairs and study in the rather nice living room.

Of course, we assumed that if Mrs. Loggie happened by and saw the necktie she wouldn't have a clue about the hidden meaning of it. And this strategy seemed to be working, that was, until one night when everything blew up.

On that particular evening, I returned from the library to our room to find the necktie in place. So, I went down to the living room to wait out the situation. Sometime later, Guati and his lady friend came down the stairs only to hear Mrs. Loggie coming out of her first floor room. At that point, because of the layout of the place, his only opportunity not to be found out was to scoot into the living room with his friend, as both of them hid behind one of the large stuffed chairs. I don't know why, but for some reason I also felt compelled to hide behind another nearby chair.

So there we were, the three of us hiding behind chairs, thinking we got away with something. When we were sure Mrs. Loggie was nowhere in the area, we came out from our chairs with Guati and his lady kind of giggling about the situation. I was quite relieved, however, thinking that we had pulled a fast one on Mrs. Loggie.

Until the next day, that was. Sometime that day when we were both occupying our room, we heard steps outside. And the next thing we knew, an envelope was being shoved under our door. That was weird. I don't recall which one of us opened it, but we shortly learned that we were being given a thirty day notice to vacate our rooms for "violation of house rules."

Obviously, we hadn't pulled a "fast one" on dear old Mrs. Loggie.

That timing was fortuitous for Guati, since summer was coming within that 30 day window, at which time he was heading back to Hermosillo anyway.

I was planning on attending classes in the summer, however. So, I managed to talk my friend Ted into joining me in an apartment on College Avenue for the summer quarter. That worked out fine financially except that Ted never made his bed (which drove me crazy, so I would make it for him), and he frequently left katsup all over the dining table, which I cleaned up. I kinda felt like his mother.

However, since the apartment was available for the summer only, I needed to find a new abode for the upcoming fall quarter when Guati would be returning. So, another search for lodging began in earnest for the fall quarter.

This time around we weren't finding anything in our price range. To make it work, we needed a third roommate to share costs.

Now, I can't recall why he was available since he was living at his fraternity house during the regular school year, but Ted agreed to share a place with Guati and me. And we managed to find a pretty nice three bedroom apartment on Arch Street, north of campus. That was great as we each would now have our own room.

It wasn't as close to campus as our previous abode but it more than made up for that with its larger environment and, best of all, no Mrs. Loggie rules about "no ladies in the house."

And no more need for neckties on the door.

7 - Sixteen Pints of Beer

Earlier I mentioned that my friend Ted shared an apartment with Guati and me. I had known Ted ever since first grade. He was a pretty bright student who was talented in many ways. And he was well liked. However, during those grammar school years and into high school, Ted and I were pretty much two students who knew each other but weren't exactly best buds. I mean, we didn't hang out together.

Then again, there weren't a lot of students that I did hang out with, save for maybe Joey DePatta, a fellow student who shared the same birth date with me, November 2, 1946. But as we grew older, Joey and I went in somewhat different directions. He took up drums, while I took up nothing beyond my studies.

I did try to learn guitar around that time, but my fingers wouldn't cooperate. So, I eventually ditched the guitar. I should have taken up piano as you'll learn I did fifty-seven years later. But better late than never.

Speaking of piano, Ted was pretty proficient at playing since he took lessons and practiced throughout his grammar school years and possibly into high school. And he was sure handy to have around when the situation called for some instrumental accompaniment. Such was the case when he joined a fraternity at Berkeley. He literally was the life of the party as he banged away at various popular tunes. I think he might have jokingly said that was the reason they took him on.

Sometimes relationships just happen, and such was the case with Ted and me. I don't really know how our friendship started except that it was around the time that Ted transferred from UC Santa Barbara to UC Berkeley. I like to think we became best friends at that point.

As noted earlier I was going to attend UCSB at one time but eventually decided Cal was for me. That was two years after I attended the University of San Francisco (USF).

With respect to Berkeley, it's not easy making friends at an institution with 30,000 students, which is kind of ironic in the first place. You can't find a friend in a place where there are another 29,999 students? Ted understood that dilemma, as did I. That's why, when he arrived at the University as a transfer student from UCSB, he rushed and eventually joined a fraternity. When I arrived at Cal, he encouraged me to join one also, preferably his. That was in my junior year.

So, I too went through the same rushing experience that he had and ultimately was asked to pledge my allegiance to his fraternity which I prefer not to name.

Once again, I must admit that I was never a social animal. As such I should have realized early on that pledging a frat house would not be in my best interests.

With my acceptance into the fraternity, I was thrown into a milieu of weekend parties where consuming large amounts of beer was an ongoing activity. This is deadly for someone like me who is prone to addiction of various sorts.

And it was at one of these parties that I had much too much hootch. Although I lost count, I would guess I had something like sixteen pints as the evening proceeded. I hate to admit it, but apparently I (I say "apparently" because that's what I was told) went out of my way to insult a hulking football player who was rushing, and he responded by nailing me to the wall. Eventually, I was "escorted" to my car and I miraculously managed to drive back to my Mitchel-Peixoto residence a few blocks away.

My friend Ted told me the story a few days later. He also acknowledged that perhaps fraternity life was not for me. He tried to be tactful, saying I was a more independent spirit. A "loner" would have been more accurate, but as I said, he was trying to be tactful. And evidently his colleagues at the frat house agreed. That was the end of fraternity life for me. It was like a divorce; I never went back to the place after that incident.

And it was likely the best thing for me. I didn't really enjoy having to be around the same guys all the time, morning, noon and night. At parties. At weekend football games. Etc., etc.

I enjoyed being "independent" too much.

Fortunately, however, this was not the end of my friendship with Ted. He still accepted me for who I was. So we continued doing many things together. Just not going to football games though.

One of those many things was a cross-country bus trip we took. Ironically enough, it was a fraternity conference in Indiana that Ted would be a part of.

So, off we went on a trip that was pretty boring at times, punctuated by stops in various towns, sometimes with interesting results.

What is most vivid, however, was the stay in Bloomington, Indiana. For the life of me, I can't recall why, but I ended up sleeping on the floor of some place. I'm not even sure if Ted stayed there as well. What I do recall is waking up, and not feeling quite right. I walked into the bathroom and gazed at a mirror. I had a rather large swelling under one eye. I mean, it was gigantic.

Shortly, Ted and another guy I didn't know took one look at me, asking how in the heck did I get such a swollen face. To make matters worse, the other guy remarked, "I think you may have been bitten by a spider." To which I replied, "Really?"

And then this guy says, "Once I saw a guy with that kind of swelling, and he didn't do anything about it." He paused.

I said, "Well, what happened to him?" To which he replied, "I heard that he died the next day."

That was enough to send me into a frenzy, with Ted commenting, "You better see a doctor."

I don't recall the details of how this situation proceeded,

but I do remember that the only doctor I could find on that weekend in Bloomington was one who handled worker's comp claims.

When I arrived at his office, I noted that there were quite a few people in his reception area. It took a while, but long story, short, I did eventually see him, and he prescribed some kind of antibiotics and sent me on my way.

At that point I decided I had enough of this cross country trip. I was dating Sally at the time and I missed her quite a bit, which gave me even more incentive to return home. Ted and I had bought tickets which would have taken us all the way to New York and back. But, at this point, there was no way I was going to continue on in that direction.

So, at this juncture of our ill-fated cross-county jaunt, I bid adieu to Ted who continued on to The Big Apple, as I proceeded to "turn tail" and run. I got the next bus I could find that was going in a western direction.

I did take one stop along the way, however. I had another friend, Danny, who was attending the Colorado School of Mines in Golden, Colorado, and was still there that summer. So, I visited with Danny and we did some local stuff, including a tour of the Coors bottling plant. That was interesting.

Next stop, San Francisco, California.

8 - The Russian Bride

There are many stories I could tell about Ted. I don't really know where to start with them. But one of those involves a period during which there were quite a few suicides on the Cal campus, with both students and non-students alike, jumping off buildings there and one who I believe actually jumped off the Campanile. I'm not completely sure that it was the Campanile, but I think it was. I think that was the point when they put a glass barrier at the top of the Campanile, however.

This is where Ted comes into the story as he told me that he was quietly walking across campus when "splat" (I think that was the exact word he used), a guy jumped from a structure landing smack-dab in front of Ted. I knew this had taken place, but it did seem somewhat coincidental that Ted was there at the time.

I'm not suggesting that Ted didn't tell the truth, but as I would find out in later years, he had a rather vivid imagination.

What's important in the saga about Ted, is that upon graduation, he did not go to law school as I thought he had planned.

In that regard, both of Ted's parents were attorneys. I think his father worked in the District Attorney's office. I know for sure that his mom taught at the Dominican College in San Rafael.

Add to that that his brother had worked for several government agencies, including both the FBI and the U.S. Marshals. And when there were terrorist threats, his brother was one of the Marshals who road shotgun on planes.

So, it goes without saying that Ted had some big shoes to fill.

I'm not sure why Ted didn't go into the law per se. Instead, he took a job as an underwriter with a local insurance company. It was a good job, but it wasn't in the law.

At some point, things began to go south for Ted. And it was probably just prior to marrying Elena, in December of 1974. And the reason I say this relates to how Ted addressed his role as best man at our wedding.

Ted did participate in the stuff related to that important point in my life, such as joining us at the bachelor's party at the Greek Taverna. Despite his participation, however, it always felt like Ted wasn't there; he was in another world, a world of his own.

An example? He was to read from a predetermined piece of scripture at the wedding, but at the last minute he appeared nervous and asked me if I would do it instead. That wasn't the

Ted I knew from the past. Not the "A" student, not the social fraternity guy, not the great conversationalist, none of that.

Which leads me to something else. And that something else made me realize that Ted was "out there" somewhere, and he wasn't coming back.

So, I'll jump to that time, about four years after the wedding, and talk about Ted and his "Russian fiancé."

I was working at the Oakland Unified School District (OUSD) when I got a call one morning from Ted in which he told me that he was getting married and asked if I would be good enough to reciprocate and be his best man.

I asked him when was the wedding, and he replied, "Today, at St. Vincent's Church." I believe it was sometime in the late afternoon.

It goes without saying, however, that I was stunned. I had no idea that he was even dating at the time. But then again, I didn't have a lot of contact with him after the wedding. Nonetheless, I dutifully left work and headed over to St. Vincent's Church which is just north of San Rafael, but a considerable drive from my OUSD job in Oakland.

When I arrived I witnessed several people I did not know, including his uncle who was a priest, and supposedly was going to officiate at Ted's wedding.

Ted looked pleased to see me and when I asked who the bride was, he told me that she came from Russia. I don't believe he told me her name. I had heard about Russian mail-order brides, however, so who was I to question his situation?

As folks continued to mill around outside the church, and when Ted wasn't in earshot, his uncle approached me and said, "When are we going to end this charade?" To which I responded, "I don't understand, Father. What's the problem?"

The priest replied, "There is no bride. It's a figment of Ted's imagination."

I stood there, flabbergasted, and could only reply, "I don't know what to do about this. Ted called me this morning and asked me to be his best man." His uncle shrugged and gave me a quizzical look.

Quite some time had passed at that point, and Ted approached me, as his uncle withdrew. I looked at Ted, wondering what was going to happen next. With a somber look on his face, Ted admitted, "I guess she's not coming today; we'll have to reschedule the wedding."

I didn't know how to respond to that, saying something like, "That's alright, Ted, let me know, okay?"

This was another turning point in my history with Ted, and one which caused me great concern. Upon leaving the Church, I went directly home (which was in Pinole at that time) and immediately told Elena about the event. She knew Ted a little from his being best man at our wedding. Fearing someday he might show up on our door step, I told Elena that if he did, she shouldn't open the door. I was very fearful he could bring harm to himself or someone else.

My memory of Ted and my relationship with him after "the wedding" that wasn't a wedding, begins to get fuzzy. Maybe it's because I was just trying to bury the whole thing. But I know I didn't make an effort to contact him after that incident.

So, time passed, until one day when I heard that Ted – who was probably only 42 years old - died at his parents' home in Kentfield. I'm not even sure how I found that out. However, the rumors were that his death was suspicious.

And that memory has haunted me ever since.

9 - Summertime Blues

When I think of summertime, I'm often reminded of Eddie Cochran's song, "Summertime Blues," and the fact that that song led to another bone of contention between Reid and my parents.

And for this we need to leave the college years momentarily, and return to the summer of 1958 when I was but eleven years old.

Later, I'll discuss the Hi-Fi record player I got when that technology came around. However, at this point I had a regular type of player when the song, "Summertime Blues" first came out. And that tune was one of my brother's favorites, but the player tended to "skip" a bit, so he took it upon himself to cure this malfunction by gluing a little penny on the arm of the player. (I'm not even sure if that solved the problem.)

When I saw what he did to my new record player, I went ballistic, and proceeded to whine to my mother that Reid had trashed my player. In turn, of course, my mom confronted Reid, telling him he shouldn't have done that without at least asking me first. And then Reid went ballistic. It was not a happy scene.

As time passed, the summers took on a more positive character. Particularly when my dad gave me a job years later in his Santa Venetia Supermarket. During the week I worked part-time in the store. It gave me a little pocket change and "kept me out of trouble." (That's meant to be a joke.)

I worked a couple of nights a week and on Saturday's, and received $1.65 an hour for my services. I did supermarket- type stuff including checking people out, stocking the shelves, and my most unfavorite role – cleaning soda pop bottles (which were surprisingly filthy) that were turned in, and loading them into crates.

During the summers, however, I worked a bit more – somewhere around 20 hours a week - if my memory serves me correctly. I met a lot of interesting people who sometimes made curious observations. Upon purchasing some type of liquor, more than one person asked me how old I was, and I responded, "sixteen years." Oftentimes, the same party would ask me how I could sell alcohol, given my age. I told them one needed to be twenty-one to buy alcohol (at the time), but that didn't apply to selling it. I'd tell them they could check with the ABC (Alcoholic Beverage Control) to learn more about that, which seemed to satisfy most of those folks.

And I was pretty good about asking for I.D. when the buyer looked like he or she could not be of legal age.

As I was saying, there were a lot of interesting people, including some who I knew from other venues. One I knew from Marin Catholic High School, who I will call "Sandra." And my father knew her and her parents and actually encouraged me to ask her out on a date. (I think that may have been the only time he would make such a suggestion to me.)

I liked this Sandra person just fine; she was very nice and also smart as a whip, but I wasn't attracted to her. She had what I would consider to be larger ankles than were necessary. I readily admit that shouldn't have been such a problem for me, but I also admit that I had a big hang-up on appearances, both my own and others.

That hang-up arose from the time I was in grammar school, when a few of my less kind classmates called me, "Big Ears." And, in all fairness, they weren't really that big, they just protruded a bit.

Their remarks were hurtful, nonetheless, to the point that one day I cryingly told my mom about it. She tried to reassure me that I was a good-looking kid, those ears would change with time, and those kids who called me names were just jealous.

But she was my mom; all moms think their kids are good looking, don't they? So her opinion didn't really count. At least from my viewpoint. I wanted others to feel that way, not just my mom.

And then one day the "Others" showed up in the form of a men's clothier in San Anselmo. This was a store that we occasionally bought my more formal attire from. I do not recall the name of the store, but one day the manager asked my mom if her son Craig would be good enough to model some clothes for boys. Of course, she knew that their interest in me would do the trick, so to speak. It was exactly "what the doctor ordered" for a boy with an inferiority complex arising from his ears.

So, of course, she told them that Craig would love to model for them. When she told me, I was thrilled and, temporarily at least, that pulled me out of my funk.

The men's store was trying to improve sales for the "younger" market. So, there I was, sitting in a studio with lighting and all that good stuff. The photographer, who worked for the local newspaper, the *Independent Journal*, asked me several times to try different poses. I began to think that maybe my appearance wasn't up to snuff and they would look for a better model.

Afterwards, however, my mom explained that the photographer told her the only reason he took so many poses was to give the store as many options as possible in selecting the pose that showed off their clothes the best. And there was another thing he told her. That was that I was so self-conscious that I wasn't smiling. They wanted a boy with smiles from ear to ear.

Ultimately, and with some assurances by the store people, I gave them those big smiles from one "Big Ear" to the next.

I was on cloud nine when my picture appeared in the newspaper shortly thereafter. There I was, wearing slacks, a nice plaid sports coat (They were the in-thing at the time.), a pink shirt (Yes, pink!) and matching tie.

And, better yet, I got to keep the coat, the shirt and the tie.

Shortly thereafter, my photo appeared in the *Independent Journal* newspaper. And it seemed like everyone at St. Anselm's School saw that picture. And weren't those mean kids jealous! From that day on no one called me Big Ears. That was, until one day about ten years later.

But that's a story in itself, one that I'll save for another episode in these memoirs.

10 - Under Whose Thumb?

Back to the subject of summer jobs.

One summer after I had started attending college at USF, my friend Phil gave me a call and suggested that I should work with him in Corte Madera.

The job involved "customer relations," taking calls from newspaper subscribers, not for the local *Independent Journal* mentioned earlier, but for the *San Francisco Chronicle*. We took calls from subscribers who didn't get their newspaper, wanted to start or stop a subscription, or any of a number of other things involving the distribution of the newspaper.

Despite the fact that you could get some pretty angry customers, the job was otherwise pretty laid back. And in many ways it was easier and less demanding than my earlier job at the supermarket.

However, the biggest attraction at that place was another student who worked there. This was the "Vicky" that I referred to earlier, and who I grew to like as much as I did Amanda during high school. Once again, I managed to get up the courage to ask her out which she fortunately accepted.

Vicky lived in nearby Terra Linda. Interestingly, she just graduated from high school and was getting ready to go to UC Santa Barbara. How ironic, given the fact that I had earlier been accepted at UCSB myself, but decided at the last minute to switch to Cal, where my friend Ted (who transferred from UCSB himself) was now going to school.

Isn't it curious, I thought, about the role that friendships can have on those kinds of decisions?

As I noted before, a similar thing happened involving my choice of USF as a post-secondary starting point.

In any case, Vicky and I dated throughout a summer which was perfectly delightful. We did everything together, going to the movies, out to dinner, day trips to various places. And we went swimming several times a week at her parents' home throughout that summer.

Now I digress. I think of Vicky sometimes, when I hear the *Stones* recording of "Under My Thumb;" at one point toward the end of that magical summer when that tune was playing, she asked me if I felt like Mick Jagger, that I had her under my thumb?

I wasn't sure if she was kidding or not, and brushed it off at the time. But maybe there was more to it than I realized. Maybe she didn't want to be under anybody's thumb.

Speaking of the *Rolling Stones*, I believe it was during the same summer that Jagger and company appeared on TV's Ed Sullivan Show. For those of you not around at that time, the group was planning on performing the hit tune, "Let's Spend the Night Together," but Sullivan's condition on that was that Mick and company substitute the words, "Let's Spend Some Time Together," since it was a family show. When they were balking at that, Sullivan told them that "either those words go, or you go."

End of discussion. After relenting, and when they were going through that number on the show with those substitute words, you could see the big grins on their faces (which appeared to say, "Isn't this really stupid?").

Now, returning to that magical summer. It was definitely the best summer of my young life. It was a wonderful time, but the downside to this affair of the heart came at summer's end when Vicky was off to UCSB and I to Cal.

I didn't know how to let go of her. I made a fruitless effort to stay in touch with her; I even suggested I could travel down to Santa Barbara for a few days to visit. I remember that particular phone call wherein she pretty much told me not to bother.

I suspected that she had already met someone else on campus who I was second fiddle to.

That was one of the two occurrences in my life when I sunk into a deep depression that I couldn't easily shake. Unfortunately, it was compounded by a concurrent case of mononucleosis that literally knocked me out with its accompanying severe fatigue.

I wondered at the time, was the mono a goodbye "gift" from

Vicky?

In any case, it was not one of my better periods in life. Starting Cal with a tough schedule of engineering and math classes, getting sick, and being depressed about the loss of my "summer love."

The whole thing went so poorly that I finally ended up seeing a shrink, who put me on the drug Lithium to get me out of my funk. It worked on the funk to some degree. But it didn't do anything for my physical health at the time.

And after two quarters at Cal, with the mononucleosis and my depression, my grades suffered, and the following Spring I was forced with leaving the University that I had had such "delusions of grandeur" about.

As I said earlier, I thought that was the end of my UC Berkeley experience until one day when my good friend Ted came to the rescue by suggesting that I should apply to Cal's School of Agriculture. So, I proceeded with a formal application to that School.

As noted earlier, the strategy worked. And in the fall I was back on campus, this time taking coursework much less demanding than my prior engineering program. After two quarters, I had racked up a nice 3.5 grade point average and was ready for the next challenge.

And this is the part I'm not so proud of. I applied for transfer to the School of Business, was accepted, and moved on to an area that would eventually pay big dividends.

It caused me to wonder what happened to that nice Dean who got me back into Cal via the School of Agriculture. Was I the straw that broke the back of the "Agricultural Camel?" Was that Dean in big trouble?

I really didn't want to think about it.

11 - "Accidents Happen"

Earlier, I related the 1958 song, "Summertime Blues," to the events of that particular time.

However, I can also relate another tune, the one from *Porgy and Bess* many years back, "Summertime," with its easy living, to those summers when I was much younger. And for the most part, those summers were quite enjoyable.

Let's return to a summer when Reid and I wished we had a swimming pool at Morningside. I'm not completely clear about the specific year, however, but Reid decided he would resolve that one day when he proudly bought and brought home a canvas swimming pool, if you could call it such. It was about two feet deep, six feet long and four feet wide. Kinda fun, but it definitely was not a real swimming pool.

Which reminds me of our going to my Aunt and Uncle's place in Sleepy Hollow where there was a real pool. They had a rather large colonial style home there, with a twelve foot high Redwood fence surrounding the real large pool (about forty feet long), along with a cabana and rest room.

At least it all seemed large to me. Maybe everything seems larger when you're young; I don't know.

So, my brother and I, sometimes with my mom, would go up to Sleepy Hollow for an afternoon of swimming and visiting with my Aunt Marce (her actual name was "Marcella"). I was quite envious at the time with respect to their apparent wealth and all that goes with that. However, I am easily impressed by things such as that; I guess you'd say I'm "impressionable."

My Aunt Marce was a very nice lady with a husband, Jack, who was a doctor and oftentimes not present since he worked a demanding schedule at a local tuberculosis hospital. I also recall that my dad wasn't terribly fond of him. I believe my father thought my Uncle was just a tad "self-absorbed." However, maybe dad was jealous of him since Uncle Jack (his actual name was "Glenroy") went through post-secondary all the way to medical school, whereas dad was the second youngest of ten children and needed to stay home and take care of his mom.

In any case, my Aunt and Uncle and daughter Elizabeth eventually left their Sleepy Hollow residence when my Uncle changed jobs. I think their next stop was Guam. I don't think my Aunt particularly cared for that place; I recall her talking about, "Geckos dropping from the ceiling." Eventually, they left Guam, with the next stop being Salem, Oregon.

Although I may have gotten that backwards, which doesn't really matter, Guam then Salem, Salem then Guam. I'm not sure of that order.

My parents and I (but not my brother who was working) traveled up to Salem to visit one summer. I think my cousin Elizabeth was not there at the time; maybe she was schooling in Europe. Again, I'm not sure. In any case, it's kind of fuzzy, but I do recall that she had a very nice Hi-Fi record player (standing for High Fidelity, a type of technology that was just emerging along with Stereo) and I decided I needed one too. I think we bought one that was similar upon our return.

Regarding Salem. While my Aunt and Uncle did not have a swimming pool at their new residence, it was still a very nice house. More importantly, I was impressed by the town of Salem itself, and the surrounding area, and thought that if we ever moved to Oregon, I'd like it to be Salem.

I digress for a moment. My Uncle Jack, unfortunately, passed away rather abruptly, in 1961, around the age of 50 years, plus or minus. I don't recall what the cause was but given his relatively young age at the time, I suspect it may have been a heart attack or stroke.

In any case, I do recall that my Aunt Marce did not take it well at all. Of course, it's difficult for anyone in that situation except that she went into a real tailspin that was noticed by just about everyone at the time.

And there likely were financial implications surrounding his death. I say this because Aunt Marce transitioned from rather exclusive surroundings, to living in an apartment in a not-very-exclusive section of San Rafael, called "the Canal." As a matter of fact, my brother Reid and his wife Gina lived there at the start of their marriage, but very shortly bought a very nice home in Novato.

Which leads me to another digression (A digression within a digression? Is there a word for that?). This second digression relates to my brother's new life with Gina. It was at a time when my parents and Reid were still in contact, before the falling out between them occurred. And, I too, was in contact with him, maybe too much contact I ultimately realized.

Why do I say this? Well, I had been his best man at the wedding. (I believe the ushers included his friend Barry Boe, Gina's brother Cesarino Bornia, and my cousin David Blake.) Anyway, being his best man, I stood in good stead with him and wished to continue our "good stead" relationship after the wedding. However, I really didn't have a good appreciation for and/or a clear understanding of the circumstances of the newly wedded couple at that point.

And why do I say that? Because I managed to show up at his apartment door-step on more than one Saturday morning, probably one too many. Being young and naïve I didn't fully comprehend that newly wedded couples don't want to be disturbed on Saturday mornings at 10 am, when they likely would be engaged in the kind of activity that such couples enjoy at that time.

After a couple of visits, with my brother in his shorts and in both cases Gina not coming out to greet me, I finally got the point.

No more Saturday morning surprises after that!

Change of subject. While I was in college, I found some pretty interesting summer jobs. Some were just okay, some were good, and some were great. One exception to the above is a summer job that was downright terrible-awful.

I think I took this job when I was living at home and going to grad school at Cal. And I don't even recall how I found it, possibly through the placement office on campus. In any case, the job was with Wells Fargo in a dreary section of San Francisco, in the dreary period of 10 pm to 2 am, and involved reconciliation of documents, one to another. That in itself was bad enough but the worst part of the job was my supervisor.

I don't recall his name, so let's just call him "Ralph." This Ralph guy was a real cracker jack reconciler. And, unfortunately, that's how he got the job of supervisor. In addition to being a cracker jack reconciler, Ralph is probably one of the best examples of the Peter Principle at its worst that one could find. If you are unfamiliar with the Principle, it simply goes like this. Ultimately, through the process of promotion, a worker will eventually reach his or her level of incompetence.

Such was the case with Ralph, who definitely was not a cracker jack supervisor. He did not know the first thing about effective supervision. As an example, when one had a problem figuring something out, and went to Ralph for help, the first thing he would do is express his disdain in the most condescending way he could. And, most often, he wouldn't even begin to show the underling how to do it right. Ralph would do the job himself, such that nobody could learn anything under Ralph. A real lose-lose situation resulting. For me, this went on for several weeks until, ultimately, I told him I could no longer work under his supervision, or lack of same, and quit.

That was the first, and fortunately the last, job that I quit on before finding a replacement job.

Probably the best one was a summer job in 1968 with an insurance firm in San Francisco. That firm was looking for business students at Cal to stand in for some of its insurance adjusters while they were away on summer vacation. I interviewed for one of those four spots and was pleased to be selected.

So, come June, there I was along with three other males – Mark, Leo and Jim - huddled together in four desks at the back of a room with a window view of the office building next door. This was fortuitous in itself because early on I could see a girl working at her desk in that adjacent building. A very attractive girl at that.

One of the other guys, Mark, noting my preoccupation with "neighbor girl," asked me when I was going to ask her out. That seemed problematic since there was no way I could converse with her under the circumstances.

That was until one day when I came up with the obvious solution. I found a big piece of cardboard on which I wrote in large lettering, "Your phone number, please?" The next thing

I needed was to get her attention. I must have stood there for the entire time of my break, about twenty minutes, hoping she would look my way.

And finally the "magic moment" arrived. She looked pretty bored at that point and was obviously taking a break herself as she looked around and then upward to our window. I looked down at her and smiled, holding up my sign for her to see.

She got the biggest smile on her face as well. She then held up her index finger in a gesture that said, "Wait a minute." Then she disappeared for a couple more minutes, but returned and held up her own sign with a phone number on it.

I was in luck!

And I didn't hesitate to call that number. She answered, and we exchanged names and agreed that we should talk further outside of work when we could be more open about ourselves and our backgrounds.

Her name was Christine.

And the rest is history. We dated that summer and into the fall. After that it was off and on over the next few years. I remember one time in particular when we had been out at a restaurant, eating and drinking. When I took her home to her parent's house in South San Francisco, her parents could tell I had been drinking and were nice enough to let me stay that night, which I did.

I had to sleep on the living room couch, however.

There is at least one unfortunate, but kind of funny, story I need to tell about that summer job.

As a substitute claims adjustor, I often took a company car to claimants' homes. On one particular trip to Mill Valley, I also took my trusty Dictaphone to record the conversation with the individual who happened to be a young girl, probably no more than twenty years old. She had an accident which was pretty much her own fault. In such cases I always tried my best to be as upbeat as possible, particularly when the person felt so lousy about their situation.

After I finished with her account of the accident she had been involved in, she was nice enough to walk me out to my company car, where I set down my Dictaphone, and continued to reassure her. I think my actual words were something like, "Please don't stress yourself. Accidents like this happen all the time."

She smiled as I got in the car and began to back up until the point that I heard a terrible crunching sound. Not sure what it was, I got out of the car only to realize what had happened when I saw the Dictaphone I had just backed over.

Yes, accidents happen to the best of us. I had a lot of explaining to do when I got back to work the next day. Of course, my three college colleagues had a good laugh at my expense.

I understand from someone else that my boss also had a good laugh with his associates when he told the story of the crunched Dictaphone.

While I'm on the subject of that summer with the insurance firm, once again, I'll address the sore subject of my "Big Ears."

There was a girl about twenty-some years old who served as the secretary to us four guys working in back. She was attractive and carefree, and a bit of a flirt at that. And she was married but that didn't stop one of the guys, Mark, from our gang of four meeting with her in a clandestine manner one weekend. And they did what young people in that situation do when they're together, of course.

The following Monday, the other three of us got a knock-down, blow by blow description of their encounter from our friend who did the deed.

Now, I'll be honest and admit that I was also attracted to her and had a hard time resisting "her charms." So, one day, the girl I'll call "Patricia," and I found ourselves in Golden Gate Park for a picnic lunch. I'm sad to say it was in the middle of a work day when we probably should have been back at our desks rather than picnicking. However, the "incident" took up only a little more than our normal one hour lunch time.

In any case, a bit after our picnic lunch, Patricia and I found ourselves in the nearby bushes doing what "younger people do in such a situation."

I'll be the first to admit it was wrong, not because it took maybe an extra half hour of our lunch time, but because she had a husband. Both my friend and I had violated someone else's turf and that just wasn't right. I don't recall whether I confessed it or not; however, it still bothered me for quite some time after the event.

So, what was the point in bringing this up? The point was it brought back memories of my grammar school years when Patricia, jokingly I think, referred to my "Big Ears." I don't really recall the exact context of her remark, but it was very hurtful. I didn't say anything; I took it in stride, but it still hurt in a way that I hadn't experienced in many, many years.

I was about ten years older than that earlier time, had some money in my bank account, and decided I was going to do something to forever rid myself of an image I disliked. Unbeknownst to my parents, or anyone else, I found a "reconstructive surgeon" in San Francisco, made an appointment, and the rest was history.

Ironically, his name was Dr. Mar McGregor. And I wondered if that "Mar" name gave anyone second thoughts about his line of work. I do recall that the good doctor, sometime later, actually made Herb Cain's column (in the *San Francisco Chronicle*) in which Cain made a similar observation.

12 - A Chance Encounter

I mentioned my girlfriend Sally earlier in the context of how my parents didn't always react positively to the choice of girlfriends made by both my brother Reid and me.

Sally was an important part of my life, very important. And it all began with a chance encounter at the College of Marin library in Kentfield, California.

This was when I had returned to Cal via the convoluted approach of admission to the School of Agriculture, only to ultimately transfer to the Business School. I had really knuckled under and by the summer of 1967, it was full steam ahead with a greatly improved grade point average. Wanting to make up for lost time, I enrolled every single quarter, including summers.

During this particular summer, I was living at home and commuting to classes at Cal, where I had a full load of coursework. I was a very serious-minded and highly motivated student, even on weekends when I would go to a nearby library to do homework and to study. My two favorite "haunts" were the Dominican College library in San Rafael, and the College of Marin library. Ted introduced me to the former where his mother happened to teach law, and I had taken summer courses at College of Marin during the previous three summers and found the library there to be a very suitable study place even when I wasn't taking courses at the College.

I digress for a moment now. (Is it my imagination, or do I seem to digress a lot?)

Anyway, as I've said more than once, there can be lots of guilt trips for persons like me, guilt trips that have their underpinnings associated with a Roman Catholic upbringing. So, at this stage of my story I'm compelled to explain the origin of my very first guilt trip.

And it also involved Sally.

Sally was a good person, a very good person. It is no doubt cliché, but I have to say they don't make people like Sally anymore. Perhaps it's due to the complexity of modern life. Or maybe it's simply because she was the person she was, raised in a family with relatively high values, albeit somewhat liberal minded. But that's likely a story in itself. So, I won't go there right now. Maybe later.

So, what happened that summer outside the College library?

If one read my first novel, *In Search of Sarah*, authored in 2015, one could get a feel for that part of my life since the novel was autobiographical in nature. For those who haven't, I'll offer the following account:

Sally and I were both in college at the time, Sally at that particular community college prior to advancing to San Francisco State University. As indicated earlier, I was pursuing my studies at UC Berkeley.

Coincidentally, we were both taking a break from studying within the College library on that Saturday afternoon. Her break was for the purpose of smoking. Being a non-smoker, my break was for fresh air.

We began a conversation, the details of which I don't recall. But I liked her immediately. And I assume she liked me. In any case, that chance meeting led to our dating each other to the point that we eventually became engaged.

The engagement itself had its origins in the "guilt trip" I am about to describe. Quite simply, I somehow managed to impregnate Sally right off the bat.

Getting her pregnant wasn't the source of the guilt trip; it was what we did about it.

We were not ready for marriage – shotgun or otherwise - given our ages and our mutual desire to complete our college education and possibly some graduate studies after that. Sally was thinking in terms of a teaching credential since she wanted to teach at a school for deaf children. I was interested in going for an MBA degree.

So we considered some options. Mine was to go somewhere else to complete our education. I suggested the University of Michigan. Of course, that implied that Sally would have the baby and we would then give it up for adoption with neither of our families being any the wiser, a very Catholic way of handling the situation.

That option certainly had its disadvantages and uncertainties. Besides Sally was not a Catholic. And while she occupied a relatively high moral ground, it did not exclude abortion which was not legal at this pre-Roe vs. Wade period of time.

At this point we had our first major disagreement: to abort or not to abort. I loved Sally and I did not want the pregnancy to come between us. So I did a very un-Catholic thing and reluctantly agreed to an illegal abortion. After all, and simply put, it was her body and her life as well.

Thus the origins of my first major guilt trip. I even confessed it in the formal environment of the Catholic sacrament of Confession.

However, the act of confession implies that one is truly sorry and would not act the same way if given another opportunity. But I honestly don't know what I would do if it happened again. Because in all such cases the other party has an equal say in the matter.

My memory is a little shaky at this point, but I believe that the priest offered some form of forgiveness along with a lecture.

This was the beginning of my falling out from the faith. Despite my confession, this decision haunted me from there on out. Part of it was the religious implication but perhaps the weightier component was what Sally went through as a result of our act.

Which next leads me to the fallout of our mutual decision.

13 - The Price We Paid

Again, what followed our decision was to some extent "documented" in my novel, *In Search of Sarah*. Except for the name changes of the various participants, the story brought forward in the novel closely parallels what actually happened when we traveled to Ciudad Juarez for an abortion by a Mexican doctor.

The "participants" included a Mexican doctor whose name I do not recall, some friends of Sally's who had coincidentally gone through the exact same state of affairs only a month earlier, and my college roommate at the time and good friend to this day, Guati.

Sally's friends provided a kind of template for what was to follow and then Guati helped to implement it by contacting the Mexican doctor they had used and setting up an appointment for "the procedure."

But the $400 procedure in 1967, an amount equivalent to over $3,000 today, did not go well. It goes without saying that although she survived the experience, it had its own consequences.

In addition to the guilt I had already incurred resulting from my part in securing the abortion, there were legal aspects that went beyond any moral considerations.

We were told that our rented vehicle was not to be taken across the border. We violated that guideline when we drove from El Paso to Ciudad Juarez. I don't really know whether that would have been considered breaking the law, however.

Nonetheless, our transgression didn't stop there. In the process of returning from our first trip across, I managed to run a red traffic light, and then to disregard a Mexican police officer who motioned us to stop. That certainly was breaking the law, probably two of them, at least as far as the Mexican police were concerned. Stupidly, I continued on, not realizing that the cop would hail another driver down and follow us.

When he caught up with us, he got into the back seat of our red Mustang and directed me to go to the police station. Unfortunately, by that time Sally was ready to pass out from what turned out to be a botched abortion.

The only good that came out of this experience was that I had just enough money to buy our way out of the predicament so that we would not end up in a Mexican jail.

But things went south from there.

That same night, upon return to our El Paso hotel room, Sally began to bleed profusely. In a panic I called the doctor. I think it was around 2 am in the morning. Fortunately, he answered the phone. When I told him what had happened, he told me to return to his clinic so that he could assess Sally's condition and take any necessary corrective action.

Once again we violated those rules about crossing the border in our Mustang rental car, arriving at the doctor's office just before the break of dawn. After examining Sally, the doctor acknowledged that there was fetal tissue remaining that needed to be removed, which he addressed.

While we were not stopped this time around, the border folks – both Mexican and U.S. - were likely a bit curious as to our crossing at the ungodly hour that we made the return trip. I was quite relieved upon our return to the hotel; however, Sally had literally been through the ringer, having to endure the two sets of procedures required to complete the abortion.

The "price we paid" included one that I could not share with Sally; she never had her own child after that experience. And to this day I really don't know whether the botched procedure she had was the cause of her not having a child.

As I earlier indicated, Sally and I eventually became engaged to be married. Had she not become pregnant and not gone through the abortion, I am unsure that we would have chosen to be engaged. With hindsight and with all due respect for Sally herself, I sometimes think that the engagement act was more a kind of recognition of a bond we shared rather than a firm commitment to be married.

I do recall our going to Granat's Jewelry Store where I bought a very nice engagement and wedding ring set that we picked out and then giving Sally the engagement ring. At that point, we began a somewhat uneasy period of engagement, not for the typical few months, but for the next several years.

We never married.

Sometime during the year 1974, Sally and I made a decision that pretty much sealed the doom for our eventual marriage. She accepted a job in southern California at a school for the deaf. I suppose I could have objected and begged her not to go, but I did not.

I think that was the event causing me to realize we would never be married.

There were periodic phone calls, letters and some trips of mine to the southland over the next few months, but otherwise we both plowed ahead with our respective careers, hers at the deaf school and mine at the University of California Office of the President.

At some point, Sally sadly informed me that she had found someone else at the school that she was serious about. I accepted her decision with some reservations, but I knew it was probably for the best, at least on her end. And I think I was happy for her.

I admittedly entered a period, not of depression, but of loneliness realizing I would never be with Sally.

Rather than wallow in that loneliness, I tried some new outlets including sailing and scuba diving. They were certainly not attempts to forget about Sally, but they were distractions of a sort.

And as with other difficult periods in my life, I turned to the bottle. Sally and I did enjoy drinking in each other's company, but this was another form of drinking. Drinking to handle this period of my life.

As I've stated more than once, I was never a social animal by nature. However, I tried to become one in a way as I found myself on Friday's after work meeting up with work colleagues at Brennan's Restaurant for drinks and social engagement.

There were several ladies that I particularly enjoyed being with. One was named Lana. I don't know if Lana or any of the others present were all that interested in me, however.

Until one Friday that was. I'll save that one for later.

Third Piece: The World of Work

1 - "You're Not Nervous?"

I was still dating Sally when I had completed my MBA program and had begun to interview firms on campus.

There was Xerox in Rochester, New York; Bechtel in San Francisco; and four or five others. I had several follow-up interviews including one with Xerox in Rochester. I didn't get a job offer from the firm but that's okay as I really didn't think I could handle the weather in that part of the country.

How did I know this? It only took one walk from my hotel to the corporate offices down the street to figure that out. Fearing I would be late for my 8 am appointment time, I walked briskly down that street, probably too briskly as suddenly I slipped on the icy sidewalk and fell on my can. Ouch! That hurt and I had a disheveled look and a soiled overcoat to prove it.

I did make the appointment on time, however. When the interviewer asked how I was doing, I explained my little fall on the street. I think the interview went downhill from there. I'm usually very prepared, maybe over-prepared for interviews, but the unsettling experience prior to the interview likely affected my demeanor and my "presentation" as well. I didn't have the requisite enthusiasm necessary to pull this interview thing off.

As I said, I didn't get a job offer from Xerox, but that was okay.

The firm I really wanted to get that elusive offer from was the international management consulting firm of A. T. Kearney & Company, Inc., which had offices all over the country and the world. And the firm was interviewing for an associate position in the San Francisco office, a locale that had the requisite climate for me.

The on-campus interview went just fine, followed by a second interview in San Francisco. Surprisingly, before I even left that place, I had a job offer in my pocket. A grand a month (quite a bit for 1971) plus excellent benefits. That package was worth about $120,000 annually in current dollars.

I couldn't have asked for more, so I accepted that offer.

I soon learned, however, that there is another important attribute that one needs to consider in the world of work, that of stability, which I will go into shortly.

In any case, the firm hired me with the understanding that my work would be entirely in hospitals and health services. The reason they hired me in the first place was because of my academic background as well as my master's thesis which focused on the economics of the nursing home industry.

Sally's father, who worked for the communications area in the State Department of Public Health, takes some of the credit for my appeal to Kearney. He needed an article on the current nursing home industry and asked me if I would take that on. I agreed and used that experience to launch my master's paper, not really appreciating its implications for my employment opportunities at the time. So that obviously paid off.

And my very first consulting assignment with Kearney was in Green Valley, Arizona, where I developed a long range plan for health services in that retirement community.

Interesting work, nice people who lived there, a good per diem, plus a bonus: several of those "nice people" would invite me over for dinner. You can't beat that! After about three months, I wrote up a report of my findings and recommendations and then was off to the next challenge.

That challenge was a hospital in Phoenix, Arizona, where I performed a study which addressed the appropriate salary and benefits package for various personnel occupations in the hospital.

Unfortunately, this is around the time that the health services well was beginning to run dry. The firm lost out on a large study which would have taken place in Chicago. That study would have kept me gainfully employed for a year or more. Without that being available, the firm had to put me somewhere else.

The first "somewhere else" was at Aerojet General in Torrance, California. I don't recall the exact nature of that engagement. However, I do recall that it was an area that I wasn't particularly familiar with.

Being the inquisitive mind that I am, I went to the Business School library at Cal and found three or four books on the subject, whatever it was. I learned a lesson in this regard, however, and that is when you adopt such an approach due to your admitted ignorance of the subject, you don't carry such books around with you.

I don't recall whether it was the VP of Kearney or someone else assigned to the project, but whoever it was, they duly noted my books and politely suggested that I don't take them with me on site. The person observed that, "Consultants are already experts in whatever they're consulting in and don't need to refer to books on the subject."

After the Aerojet engagement, and still with no health services work available, I assisted another senior consultant in developing what was called a "unit train." It was interesting but not really in my field.

Once that work was finished, I found myself sitting at my desk in the San Francisco office of A. T. Kearney & Company.

Consultants are not supposed to sit at their desks for any extended period. They're supposed to be out in the field working on billable projects, and only sit at their desks when they write their reports.

So, day after day, I sat doing various busy-work for other consultants, most of which was unbillable.

To make matters worse, the vice president of the SF office would walk by my desk every day he was in the office saying something like, "You're not getting nervous, are you?"

In my naivete, I took this as a form of consoling, not completely understanding the true meaning behind that remark.

And so I would ultimately learn that pleasantries such as, "You're not getting nervous, are you?" are not meant to be consoling, rather they're code for otherwise saying, "You're looking for another job, aren't you?"

And no, I wasn't looking for another job when I obviously should have been. After a few weeks of "not being nervous," the VP finally called me into his office to inform me that there was no more health services work in the foreseeable future, and I was given a measly one week notice of my being laid off.

It wasn't the end of the world. I lived at my parents' home all this time when I wasn't on the road; they didn't charge me rent which was very considerate of them. And on top of that I saved quite a bit of money based on my generous salary and benefit package. The worst part of this experience was the resulting loss of self-esteem felt by one who is not gainfully employed.

The best part, however, was the lesson that was learned: the work world can be a rocky one, and there are no guarantees of continued employment (unless you have a contract saying otherwise) when things don't go well.

My dad learned that lesson years ago.

Now it was my turn.

2 - Another Chance Encounter

Earlier I mentioned that on Fridays, at Brennan's Restaurant in Berkeley, many of my colleagues at the UC Office of the President would meet for drinks and conversation. I knew most of these folks who worked on the same floor as I. On a particular Friday, however, I believe in the month of June of 1974, I met someone new, someone that I hadn't already known. And she seemed to command my attention.

Her name was "Elena." That was the name she went by, anyway. Her full name was "Maria Elena Rosales." Although members of her family called her "Nena."

So, what was different about Elena? She actually paid attention to me, unlike some of the others. Or at least, acted like she was interested in what I had to say. It was human nature; I couldn't help but react positively to her.

But in reflection I could ask myself, was I attracted to Elena because she was who she was, or was it because I desperately missed Sally and needed someone else to take her place? I like to think it was the former.

It went beyond her merely paying attention to me. She checked all the boxes this time around. There were attributes similar to those of Sally, but there were others as well.

She came from a good family, like Sally.

She had a pleasing personality, like Sally, but in a different way.

She was Roman Catholic, unlike Sally.

I thought she was attractive in appearance, the same as Sally but again in a somewhat different way.

And as I said, she was a good listener, perhaps just a bit more than Sally.

She was available, similar to Sally when I met her, but maybe a little bit more so because of her personal situation.

On that last count, Elena was recently divorced. Her "ex" had been unfaithful, so she filed papers for dissolution, and in so doing, took control of her situation and was, once again, open to dating. In that respect, we were both going through a "divorce" of sorts.

The "pairing" of the two of us had other parallels with Sally. Within a short period, we were engaged. But this time the engagement actually led to marriage within only six months.

I do recall that at the time I proposed marriage, Elena asked if I were concerned about the age difference since she was a few years older than me. I responded that it was fine since women tend to outlive men anyway; the age difference would actually work in our favor, decreasing the likelihood of one of us spending years without a partner when that partner is gone.

I think she appreciated my take on the situation.

However, soon the differences in our personalities and values began to emerge. Some good, some not so good. She was disappointed when I noted, after the fact, that our December wedding should have been put off until the new year because of the tax advantages. To Elena our timely marriage superseded any financial considerations such as taxes.

And there were other differences, some more substantial than others. She was fiercely loyal, or perhaps a better word, faithful, unlike me. I thought I too was loyal and faithful, but I was to learn eventually that those qualities, if they existed in me at all, could be easily challenged.

And there would be more than one individual that would cause that to happen.

The first person I'll call "Eleanor."

3 - Career Moves

Early on in my career, I changed jobs frequently. About once every four or five years. I was always on the lookout for the next big opportunity to advance myself. (See Exhibit III for professional employment record.)

As I said earlier, I was working as a senior analyst in the Office of the President of the University of California, when Elena and I first met. That job was definitely not one of the more enjoyable or rewarding ones in my life. There were a lot of big egos lurking in that place during the six years I was there. Very few folks that I cared to be with outside of work.

I'll return to that aspect a little later. As a matter of fact, it would not be an overstatement to say the job drove me to the bottle. In addition to the Friday after-work meetups at Brennan's, I would continue that drinking experience at home. But as one of my apartment neighbors not so charitably told me, I shouldn't be drinking alone which he found me at oftentimes when he'd knock on my door. Of course, neighbor Ben also took advantage of that situation by inviting himself to then drink in my presence, which he said was just fine because we were doing it together, of course. Sly Ben.

However, for better or for worse, that was the beginning of an off-and-on period in my life where indulging in alcohol was an all too common experience.

Back to the subject of work. I left University employment to take what turned out to be a short-term experience with an aerospace company in San Rafael, California, called Aerojet Composites. Coincidently, the company was a subsidiary of Aerojet General (which I had consulted for), that had recently bought it out. It was not a large company, about twenty employees in total. As the title suggests, it was involved in the fabrication of composite plastics for the aerospace industry. There were two partners in charge of the company, one I liked a lot and the other was a so-so kind of guy.

While the job was one of my more enjoyable ones, unfortunately, the parent company was not getting the contracts that could continue to support the subsidiary.

Shades of A. T. Kearney.

At that point, my job shifted dramatically, going from administering contracts to handing out pink slips to the fabrication workers. The company would eventually go belly up. My boss kept me on as long as he could afford to, thinking that big contracts would shortly be coming our way.

Until one day when he finally realized that wasn't going to happen. Then I was the unfortunate party getting the pink slip.

At that point I couldn't be picky about my next source of employment since I had a wife and two children, Matthew and Jeffrey, to support. So I grabbed the first job offer that came along from the Oakland Unified School District which turned out to be the second most political job experience I would ever endure (the first will be discussed in a future episode). But I persevered, and even managed to advance myself in the face of those political experiences as I learned that sometimes with politics came opportunities. Unfortunately, my poor boss was on the losing end when he was replaced by me taking on his old job. They then moved him to "special projects." That was difficult for me since he was a good person who I was quite fond of.

So, I had gone from principal budget analyst when I was hired, to chief of budgetary planning (which was a title I created in the advancement process).

After the departure of Oakland Superintendent Ruth Love (who took a similar position in the Chicago School System), there was quite a bit of turnover at my bosses' level, the assistant superintendent of business services (also referred to as business manager), around that time. I believe I had at least four different bosses while I was at the District.

At that time Love's deputy, Charles Mitchell, accompanied her to Chicago, telling me as he left that he would get back in touch about my taking on the budget director position in Chicago. I had mixed feelings about that. Admittedly, that job paid double what I was earning, but I had heard that Chicago was ripe with politics, even more so than Oakland.

As it turned out I didn't have to deal with that possibility when very shortly Mitchell became mired down in Chicago politics, losing his job in the process.

After but eighteen months as chief of budgetary planning, the next business manager suggested to the new superintendent, David Bowick, that I be promoted to "interim business manager" as he was leaving to take another job himself. So, accepting his recommendation, Bowick appointed me to the position of assistant superintendent in charge of business services. In that position I supervised several individuals who were much older than I. And I don't think they were all that happy about the situation.

But what could I say? I had worked hard to move up the ladder.

That was until the progression ended when I was passed over for the permanent position. When I inquired as to why I missed out on that opportunity, I was told that the successful candidate had a doctoral degree. It was at that point I decided I, too, needed a doctoral degree if I were serious about getting ahead in the field of educational administration.

That explains why my next stop was with the Orinda Union School District where I took on the business manager position for a little over four years with the understanding that I would pursue my doctorate with USC at its Sacramento Public Affairs location during that period.

I had negotiated a very good contract with the District, one which allowed me to seek the next career opportunity when I ultimately completed my doctoral studies. At that point I was looking for a job in the community college sector where there would be new challenges and more money.

Working forty plus hours a week, raising a family and making trips to Sacramento for four days of classes every month began to take a toll, however, on both me and Elena.

And while Elena accepted the requirements of my program, she likely didn't share my enthusiasm over the trips to Sacramento for classes, an essential part of that program.

Besides those monthly absences, some of my class members held ongoing meetings as a study group at our homes. Those members included an attractive lady living in a nice hillside house in Mill Valley that she had acquired as a result of her divorce from her lawyer husband.

Although Elena had never met this particular classmate of mine who I will call, "Sheila," I believe she may have conjured up some rather distressing thoughts about the lady. While there was nothing at all going on between myself and Sheila, I probably talked her up a bit more than was wise at the time. As a result, this added one more strain to our marriage.

Ironically, the real target of Elena's negative feelings at that time should have been directed toward my secretary, who I will call "Eleanor." Eleanor provided the support I so dearly needed at that critical time, both practical and emotional. As a result, I fell into a relationship all too common for men in my particular situation.

I admit that I was wrong in seeking or accepting the kind of support that a person like Eleanor provided. I am not trying to justify the relationship, but only to explain how it came about and the added pressure it put on our marriage.

It would be a lie if I were to suggest that Eleanor came on to me. I certainly shared responsibility for the relationship that evolved slowly over a period of three or four years while I was working in Orinda.

Furthermore, I am reluctant to put any blame on my boss at that time. However, it is only fair to the situation to note that the superintendent herself was very demanding and not necessarily the most fun person to work for. And as a coworker, Eleanor was better able to understand the situation than anyone else. Not only did she understand the things that were gnawing at me, but she also tried to make my work life a bit better during those years while I was pursuing my degree and working forty plus hour weeks. She never hesitated to take on anything that would make a difficult day a better day for me.

There was a clear turning point in the evolution of my relationship with Eleanor. It came about when the school district was organizing an educational field trip to the northern coast on a work day. The director of the program was nice enough to invite me to join the group that day. (Probably realizing that the person in charge of her budget might look more favorably at her program with an on-the-job experience.) I, in turn, asked if it would be okay for Eleanor to join us which the director said was just fine.

What were my motives?

Frankly, I enjoyed Eleanor's company and also wanted to reward her for her diligence in providing the support that she lent to that particular program director.

But again, in all honesty, I was also looking for an opportunity to be with Eleanor outside of work. So off to the coast we went on what was a pretty nice spring day. Without going into the details, Eleanor and I found ourselves alone on a beautiful beach with a picnic lunch. And while nothing untoward happened on that beach, it was the beginning of a close friendship between the two of us.

The program director never saw the likes of us that day. And again the old RC guilt kicked in as I used work as an excuse to have a pretty nice day by spending time with my secretary, something that could be hurtful to Elena who I still loved very much. Some, including Elena herself, would question how I could have a relationship with another person and still claim that I loved my wife.

But I did, nonetheless.

And again, without going into details, for the remainder of my employment in Orinda, Eleanor and I would continue to maintain the bond that we shared.

However, we both realized that our situation would change dramatically when I graduated from my doctoral program and then moved on to the next challenge.

And I would miss her.

4 - More Career Moves

The end of my contract with the District was fast approaching, and I was sending out my feelers seeking more "career advancement" opportunities.

Most of those opportunities were with community colleges at the vice president level. And it seemed for a time like I was attracting more letters of rejection than I would have liked. I learned it's not easy to break into a system in which you are not currently employed.

After about six months of community college interviews, sometimes with follow up visits, but always without any offers of employment forthcoming, I finally landed a follow-up interview combined with an offer of employment from the Merced Community College District.

The Merced area would not have been my first choice of locale for a new job. However, as it turned out, the job itself was the best administrative position of my career.

Great boss. Actually, two great bosses in succession when the first left to take on the presidency at a large multi-college district down in Orange County. I had a great secretary (who I did not have a personal relationship with) named Dee. Great subordinates as well.

I fondly recall one of them, named Marvin, who was my finance director. He was a neat guy, both inside and outside work, although the president didn't appreciate him quite as much as I did, largely because of his personality "quirks."

Marvin persuaded me to join him and some others for a pick-up basketball game more than once.

Why do I remember those games? I happen to have a damaged pinky as a result of Marvin's overly enthusiastic defensive coverage of me when our hands collided as I drove to the basket. Ouch! That hurt a bit. Probably should have gone to a doctor and got it set properly, but I didn't.

So, whenever I look at my left hand pinky, I think of Marvin's gusto for things basketball-wise, bless his soul. Unfortunately, Marvin passed away a few years ago. He wasn't that old. Maybe in his sixties. I was very sorry to hear about that.

Back to Merced. Lovely town with numerous opportunities for civic engagement encouraged by my first superintendent boss. Very encouraged, as a matter of fact. You name it, there I was. Rotary Club President-elect, Leadership Merced program, Chamber of Commerce, among others.

I even had an opportunity for a part-time teaching assignment when the one of the officers associated with Golden

Gate University hired me to teach a budgeting and finance course at Castle Air Base.

During my stay at the Merced District there were things that were thrust on me and there were others that I took on with great enthusiasm.

One most memorable experience was being able to participate as one of the sixteen members of the UC Merced Campus Committee, a group of local politicos who were lobbying for the next site for a campus of the University of California. The second president was at the District Office at the time. I needed to "lobby" a bit with her to take on this particular role.

It was a natural fit for me since I had formerly worked at the central office of the University, was an alum of UC Berkeley, worked at the local community college and tried to maintain as many ties as possible to the University.

Each member of the committee had a specialty and mine was in academic planning wherein I offered the related reasons why Merced itself was best equipped to become the tenth campus of the University.

Unfortunately, I left the Merced area and the Committee itself just before the work of that Committee was wrapped up. However, I was gratified that Merced was eventually successful in its efforts when I learned that the UC Regents awarded it with the University's tenth campus. And from my perspective it was a fitting tribute to the five years of life and work in that central valley town which my family and I grew to love during that brief time.

And Merced's success in being the next campus of the UC system also came at a time when I had just achieved my own goal of working in a multi-college district, having been hired as the associate chancellor for the San Mateo County Community College District (SMCCCD), a three-college district.

It was a bitter-sweet experience since my family was perfectly satisfied with life in Merced. And I was as well. As I said I had great subordinates and I enjoyed all the various activities that I had been involved in while I was in Merced.

One of my subordinates, my bookstore manager, Frances, who I was very fond of, asked why I wanted to leave Merced College. I tried to explain my motives relating to advancement as well as returning to the SF Bay Area, but she really wondered if it was the right move for me.

With hindsight I think she may have been spot-on as to whether it was the right decision at the time. I would shortly learn that San Mateo was just as political as Oakland, maybe more so, at least with respect to the administration itself. From the get-go I didn't have the same warm fuzzy feeling in the new multi-college district as I had with Merced.

One of the reasons was undoubtedly because I took over from a lady who had literally "grown up" in the SMCCCD. And there were frequent references to how she did things differently from me.

It was an uphill battle for the next eight years as I tried to chart a course based on my fifteen years of experience as an educational administrator not always getting the desired support from my subordinates, as well as my boss. I found myself working through lunch time and after hours and weekends more and more. And once again there was a resulting strain on my family and my marriage.

Nonetheless, I did have one supporter among my subordinates.

And that's a story in and of itself.

5 - Organizational Politics

Yes, getting a senior management job in a multi-college district certainly had been a goal of mine, and after applying to and interviewing in several such districts, I had finally achieved that goal with my hire as the associate chancellor (AC) for the San Mateo County Community College District.

The District covered the area from San Bruno down to Redwood City, and included three colleges: Skyline College, the College of San Mateo, and Canada College, with enrollments of over 40,000 students.

The former occupant of the AC position had recently retired. And as I already noted, she was a hard act to follow. She had worked in the District just about her whole working career and had been in that AC position for almost twenty years.

Her former subordinates weren't used to having anyone else beyond this person giving them direction. And more than once in the course of that direction, one of her former minions seemed compelled to tell me "how Ruth did it." I would bite my lip when someone made that observation, but it wasn't easy.

Nonetheless, I always did what I thought was the right thing under the circumstances. And in the case of the SMCCCD, one of those was a reorganization of the business services area for which I was responsible. Not only did it result in an outcome that I thought was best for that area, but I also ended up promoting more than one person in the process. In my own naïve way, in addition to efficiency considerations, I also thought that these changes would buy me some good will from those subordinates who were having some difficulty transitioning from Ruth's oversight to mine.

But that wasn't the way things played out.

It may have had just the opposite effect, causing some in-house jealousies to arise.

There was no manager for the area of budget, an area that requires careful oversight. So I reorganized staff such that an individual who formerly was in charge of accounting, who I will call "Laura", took on the new position of budget director.

Next, I promoted the person who had been responsible for purchasing, Rhonda, into a broader financial position, which included an area formerly in Laura's purview.

As things would have it, Rhonda not only took on her new role rather well, but she also became a key supporter of mine, not because she had been promoted, but because that was her nature, to support "the boss" whether it was Ruth or the new guy on the block.

While I certainly appreciated that support, it was likely the source of tension between her and Laura as well as jealousy coming from Laura as well as others.

Here I learned a valuable lesson: if you appreciate a person's loyalty and support, try not to demonstrate it in ways that will call attention. Having said that, however, I don't know that it would have made much of a difference at SMCCCD because of the nature of the individuals involved and their pre-existing loyalties to other players in the work environment.

This is not to say there were no positives in the work environment. There were and so I will tell a story which highlights one of them. In a later episode of this work I will discuss my so-called "vehicular life," chronicling all of the automobiles I've had the pleasure of owning. One of those being my '96 Porsche 911 Cabriolet which I purchased after being with the District about four years. It was a real beauty, Torch Red exterior color, and beige interior leather upholstery. Also with a manual transmission that made driving that car all the more fun.

So, one day when the staff were making one of their trips to a local restaurant for lunch, I tagged along for a change. (I didn't do lunch all that much, oftentimes working through it and eating at my desk which was not a good habit, I admit.)

In any case, when we were leaving that restaurant I was in the company of Rhonda and my secretary Lolly. Again, trying to "upgrade" my relations with staff I tossed my key fob to Lolly and told her she could drive my Porsche back to work.

Of course, this caught her completely by surprise but she willingly took the fob and drove the car back. I think she was thrilled.

And it was a kind of recognition for what she and Rhonda had done earlier. They had given me a neat "flat cap," sometimes referred to as a "newsboy" made of Burberry material. They thought that it would be appropriate for me when my Cabriolet top was down and the wind was blowing my hair.

And in all fairness, my giving the fob to Lolly was more than an attempt to "upgrade." I really appreciated their thoughtfulness and wanted to show that appreciation in some tangible way.

Having said that I will move on.

After five or six years and turnover in the chancellor level, the prevailing politics moved from administration to the Board of Trustees. The new chancellor hadn't hired me so there was not the same commitment as I had from the former chancellor. Things were going on behind the scene that caused that Board, which I formerly thought I stood in good stead with, to become aware of my relations with staff, relations which were admittedly not as good as I would have liked, and had also increased the level of tension both inside and outside my office.

I never knew exactly what was going on between the new chancellor and the Board he served, since I believe it was "filtered" to me by the chancellor himself. While I would accept what I was told by my superior at that time, frankly I didn't always believe what he said.

One thing was clear, however, he was attempting to placate the Board. Less charitably I would observe that he was trying to cover his own ass while my relations with subordinates were worsening with the Board becoming more aware of those worsened relations.

Ultimately, I was moved from my AC position to a parallel position as AC for fiscal policy and planning and was given a new assignment which involved overseeing the Board's desire to pass a tax measure for the purposes of upgrading facilities at the three college district. At that point, my office moved from the first floor up to the second and I went from supervising an area of more than thirty employees to one with zero staff. This wasn't what I had in mind when I first came to San Mateo. But at least I still had a job.

Unfortunately, that measure failed to pass for which I definitely will not take responsibility. From my perspective the chancellor himself failed to devote sufficient energies to pass a measure that the public clearly was not yet ready for. Further, he failed to orchestrate the kind of studies that would have forewarned him of that outcome. (Four years down the road, a similar measure would pass under a different leader.)

If it had passed I would have been involved in the implementation phase of the tax measure, but without that outcome, I became excess baggage for the District.

Although I didn't realize it at the time, shortly I would learn that there was light at the end of the tunnel.

6 - A New World

Things had come to a turning point, and I likely could have been fired if I hadn't had a stipulation in my contract for a full-time position as full professor at one of the colleges should things go south. So, after conferring with the Board, the Chancellor implemented that part of the contract. (For a complete academic employment record see Exhibit IV.)

At first I taught at two of the colleges – Skyline College and College of San Mateo – which led to a full-time position at the latter a year later.

More importantly, I finally found my niche in the world of education, teaching courses in business, management, project management, and organizational behavior. And the doctoral degree finally paid off in terms of not only my qualifications to teach, but also with an added stipend on top of my professorial salary which admittedly wasn't anywhere near what I had been making in my administrative position. But that was okay, I finally was being paid for doing something that I enjoyed very much and without the pressures of managing or the petty jealousies arising in the administrative environment.

Of course, even though I was "gifted" with the professor position, like everyone else I needed to go through a formal evaluation. In addition to other faculty and the college dean herself, my evaluation extended to students as well. With positive reviews coming from all directions, I went through the required review period successfully and was granted tenure at its conclusion.

A slight sigh of relief at that point. I now could concentrate on doing the best job I could to help prepare students for the world of work or, in other cases, transfer to a four-year institution. I took my new assignment quite seriously, holding office hours as needed, serving on committees, all in addition to my teaching assignment of five courses every semester.

I taught both day and evening classes and to some degree enjoyed the differences in my student "clientele" with the day classes comprised mainly of younger students and the evening with older students and those who worked. I could particularly appreciate the latter group since at one time, I too was working and going to school myself. And I still have fond recollections of many of my students, several of whom chose to take additional courses from me as it fit with their fields of interest.

I even managed to attract a few employees from the District office to take my courses. That was one of the upsides of that former experience and it told me that I had a support group in administration that I was never really aware of. Those clearly were the staff who were devoted to their jobs and chose not to get involved in office politics. And several of them also took additional courses from me, some stating that I was the best professor they had taken classes from.

I can honestly say that the ten years I spent teaching at the colleges were the best years of my career. Both during and after that time, I asked myself why I never took on a teaching role earlier in my career. And sometimes when I think about my particular world of work, I wonder how things might have turned out differently in other facets of my life had I never gone into administration. That's a kind of "what if" question akin to Hugh Everett's "many worlds theory."

Maybe somewhere, somehow, there's a Craig Thomas Blake who went into teaching after receiving his doctoral degree and had a happy and a rewarding life from that point on. A life with no alcohol, no drugs, an enjoyable occupation and one surrounded by an understanding and supportive environment.

Is that an unrealistic quest? And if I had an opportunity for a "do-over" is that the path I would have chosen?

Yes, in a heartbeat.

7 - Reaching Out to Reid

It's now been exactly ten years since a major event in my life and someone else's took place. And as I have mentioned more than once, my brother Reid and my parents had a falling out over the years. Unfortunately, it was one that I also got sucked into. It's not easy to take sides in such circumstances. If you do, it's also a no-win situation. As it turned out, my allegiance was with my parents for better or for worse. I did not see Reid for many, many years. I can't even begin to say how long that was, but it was definitely too long.

When Rhonda and I were living at the Half Moon Bay townhome, I began to look at the situation through a different lens. Maybe it related to my mom passing on so there were no parents to deal with anymore. Maybe it was because I had just retired and had a bit more time on my hands. I really don't know. But I do know that I discussed the situation with Rhonda and we agreed that it was time for me to "mend some fences" with Reid and his wife Gina.

As a result I decided to write Reid a letter which started out by explaining that I almost died two years earlier and that I had been given a "second chance in life and I'm not going to waste it." I went on to tell him that I loved him and missed not having him in my life. In that letter I acknowledged what he had meant to me over the years and how we were living parallel lives with both of us having two boys among other things. I told him that Rhonda and I would love to take him and Gina to dinner to celebrate his 70th birthday.

Reid responded very positively to me in a telephone conversation during which he told me that he never felt any ill will toward me. We had an extended conversation about many things, the conversation lasting well past an hour. We agreed to meet for dinner at San Rafael Joe's restaurant, kind of a "mid-point" between his residence in Novato, and our place in Half Moon Bay, on Wednesday, July 13, 2011. I am able to call up this specific date since I kept some notes on our reunion.

Other aspects of our reunion, I'm unable to readily pull up, but there are some highlights I do recall.

The first and perhaps most important was what Gina ultimately referred to as "the book." This was actually an album that I put together for the occasion. It included pictures over the years of Reid and me and others. Every page had text which described some significant event in our lives.

And then there were other activities that took place after the first meet up at Joe's.

At the time I was also trying to put together a larger reunion of the Blake family relatives. Many still lived in Minnesota. Others had come to California over the years. On my end were cousins David, Roger, Cece, Elizabeth, Vickie, and of course, Reid and me and all of our children and grandchildren.

Back in Minnesota were aunts and uncles, and more cousins. The oldest member back there was Aunt Marie, who I believe had just turned 97 years of age.

I managed to convince my sons Matt and Jeff to be available for a reunion in Minnesota on a given date. And I believe Cece and her husband Ken were going to make the trip. I couldn't track down Elizabeth, and David bailed on us.

As it turned out, however, there wasn't quite as much enthusiasm on the part of the Minnesota clan as on my end. If I correctly recall, Cousin Pam was concerned about Marie participating due to her age. I actually talked to Aunt Marie on the phone for over an hour and she seemed just fine to me. The clincher was that Pam wasn't able to find an appropriate place in their area for a reunion.

So, the "large family reunion" began to fall apart at that point, which was very disappointing to me.

Nonetheless, Rhonda and I continued to organize "get togethers" with Reid and Gina and their family. The one where everybody was present was held at their home. Their sons, my nephews, are Scott and Steven. The two of them have four children of various ages. Scott and his wife Connie have a son and a daughter named Garret, and Courtney respectively, while Steven and his wife Debbie also have a son and daughter named Trent, and Taylor respectively.

The party was very successful. There was swimming in the pool and a barbeque and the kids had a lot of fun. Jeff and Loree brought their two children, Eli and Camdyn, who were quite small at the time. Matt and Jamie brought their sons Jake and Noah. Their son Griffin was not part of the family yet.

I fondly recall almost all of the children playing in the pool together. Lots of laughing and yelling and kids doing all kinds of pool type stuff. It was a great opportunity, particularly for the kids to meet and play with each other.

There were other events involving Reid and Gina. We had them over one Saturday to give them a tour of Half Moon Bay which we all enjoyed.

Also, this was a time when I had been going to the drag strip in Sonoma with my Camaro. So I invited Reid to join me and we went together to Sonoma. It was a reverse of times when Reid would take me to the drag strip fifty years earlier.

Another memory comes to mind. When I wrote my first novel, *In Search of Sarah,* late in 2015, I told Reid and he asked for a copy which I sent to him. He liked to read. He told me at the time that he was reading a western novel. When he received my novel in the mail on a weekend, he told me he put his western novel down and then proceeded to read mine. He readily admitted that he wasn't an aficionado of science fiction, but he made an exception in his reading tastes in this case since as he said, "I know the author." He managed to polish that book off over that weekend.

Unfortunately, that was the last communication I had from my brother.

On or around January 30 of the year 2016, his son Scott called to tell me Reid had just passed away.

I was taken totally aback by this since Reid was very active and appeared to be in good health. Nonetheless, one morning he got up, went to the bathroom, and suddenly had a heart attack.

On reflection, I wish I had known he had a heart condition; I would have told him to see a doctor. However, my understanding is that he rarely saw one and probably didn't have annual physicals.

He died at age 74, the same age I am presently.

Fourth Piece: Leisure World

1 - Approaching Retirement

Things change considerably when one leaves the world of work behind, whether it is the life one lived or the one that is remembered (since memories aren't always accurate as one grows older).

For me the changes began to take place after May 4th of the year 2010, when I was presented with the District's form of a "gold watch," a plaque stating that this "Distinguished Service Recognition" is awarded to Craig Blake "in acknowledgement of eighteen years of dedicated service as a member of the College Faculty (It was actually ten years but they included my time in administration whether purposely or by mistake), with best wishes for many years of health and happiness in retirement."

Was my service really distinguished? Or were those just words that were fashioned for retirees in general? I won't question it at this point; I'll just accept it for what I would like to think was the case in my particular situation. Whether it was ten years or eighteen years, it doesn't really matter that much. Those years comprised a big chunk of my time in the world of work.

That distinguished service recognition marked a new period in my life. The path was chosen, much as the words of the marriage contract dictate, "for better or for worse." And having chosen that path, I was on a new course and would need to deal with the cards that I was dealt, no matter how good or bad those cards were.

As with the prior ten years or so, this period was without my marriage partner of almost twenty-five years. When I moved out of our home in Eagle Trace in Half Moon Bay, I first lived alone in each of two apartments in the Burlingame hills. That was where I was residing when something horrific in nature, referred to as "9/11," occurred on the other side of the country.

If someone happens to read this memoir long into the future, or lived in a cave at the time, "9/11" is a reference to the date, September 11, 2001, on which there were a series of coordinated attacks by a terrorist group known as "Al-Qaeda." On that Tuesday morning four commercial airliners were scheduled to land in California. However, in mid-flight, they were hijacked by 19 terrorists. As a result, two of the planes were redirected to New York City where they crashed into the north and south towers of the World Trade Center in the City. And shortly both towers collapsed.

A third flight hijacked over Ohio was crashed into the west side of the Pentagon.

According to reports at the time, the fourth and final plane was initially flown toward Washington, D.C., but crashed in a

Pennsylvania field after a struggle between passengers and the terrorists.

Our country, led by President George W. Bush at that time, formally responded by launching a war on terror in Afghanistan to depose the Taliban which had not complied with the U.S. demands to expel the Al-Qaeda from Afghanistan and extradite their leader Osama bin Laden. Little did Bush realize then that the "war on terror" would continue on for twenty years thereafter.

The destruction of the World Trade Center seriously harmed the New York City economy and caused a crash in stock markets worldwide.

Trading on Wall Street was closed from that day on through September 17.

And I clearly recall that day, when after hearing about this monumental disaster, I called Elena to see if she was alright. There was really no reason for me to be concerned about her since she was 3,000 miles away from what had happened, but I was somehow compelled to do that. I don't think she shared my feelings of concern and seemed somewhat bewildered by my call.

I guess that such feelings of concern aren't always reciprocal.

I was still living in that Burlingame apartment when Elena bought a townhome in Martinez around the year 2002. As a result of our separation and the related division of assets, Elena had more than adequate funds for the purchase of her new home which, admittedly, was a small one bedroom unit.

I was happy for her at the time. She certainly deserved to have something to call her own.

And up until that point I was quite satisfied with my Burlingame apartment; however, her purchase was an impetus for me to do likewise. I asked myself: why did I want to pay rent when I could do as Elena did and invest in my own home?

Realizing the relatively high prices in most of the Bay Area, I opted to return to Half Moon Bay (a more affordable venue) where Elena and I had our last home, to buy a reasonably priced townhome in a small enclave called Cyprus Cove near the entry to HMB.

The home was about 1,700 square feet in size, plus a two car garage, and had four levels with stairs of only about seven each leading up to the next level. At my age of fifty-five this was quite manageable. Perhaps it would be less so at my current age of seventy-four, I'm not really sure. In any case, early on I went about the task of decorating my new abode.

I particularly recall my attempt to place some attractive fake plants on a kind of overhang about sixteen feet above the entry way. I used a rather long extension ladder to accomplish this form of decoration. Stupidly, I placed the ladder against the wall upside down which meant that the intended supports at the foot of the ladder were not placed correctly. No sooner than I had reached the very top rung of this ladder, it decided that it no longer chose to support me and went sliding across the floor, taking me with it all the way down.

Ouch! I would never do that again! It managed to leave me with some very damaged toes in the process, toes which always remind me of that particular experience.

I no longer climb ladders. I leave that to the person who became my partner in life, Rhonda.

2 - My Vehicular Life

My narrative would be incomplete if I didn't address my love of things vehicular and the cars I've owned over the years. At least incomplete from my perspective, that is.

As noted earlier, my first automobile was the '56 Pontiac Catalina that my mom was good enough to turn over to me when I was sixteen years old and had just acquired my first driver's license.

That license wasn't a particularly easy thing to acquire. And I had been forewarned about one of the "examiners" that might oversee my "behind the wheel" portion of that process. My Aunt Marce was tested by a guy named "Stoddard" and the fact that I remember this person's name is indicative of the impact the driving exam had on me. Aunt Marce told me he was a real "son-of-a-gun" or some similar uncharitable reference. (And I'm using his real name because he's likely long gone at this point.)

There was more than one examiner at the Department of Motor Vehicles (DMV), but it was my bad luck to also draw the Stoddard card on the day I showed up for my exam. So you don't have to wonder about that outcome further, I'll say that I ultimately passed the test, but it was by a whisker. And it all came down to just one little portion of the test. I had successfully performed the parallel parking maneuver. I obeyed all the various signs we encountered on the way. I gave the proper hand signals for turns (they wouldn't let you rely on your automated turn signals). And so on and so forth.

The nail that almost sealed the coffin on my driving exam involved a simple direction he gave to me. He told me to "take the next turnoff" while we were driving down the "miracle mile" toward San Anselmo. (The joke about this road was that it was a miracle if you survived the entire mile or so).

In any case, it would be a miracle if I survived the Stoddard exam itself as I passed an immediate turnoff to go to the "next" turnoff. At this point, he became fairly belligerent, asking me why I didn't take the turnoff as instructed. My retort was, "You said to take the 'next one,' didn't you? This is the next one."

He became even more belligerent at that point saying, "No, this turnoff you took was not the next one, it was the one after the one you should have turned off."

Not trying to be a wise guy, I replied, "It's semantics. I didn't interpret your instruction the way you wanted me to." Rather than saying anything else, he went, "Humph!" and proceeded to write something on my score sheet that likely wasn't very good.

After we had pulled into the DMV parking lot, he continued to make notations on his notepad as I awaited my fate. I don't recall exactly what he said, but it wasn't very pleasant. Then he finally said something to the effect of, "You passed the driving exam, but you really need to work on your turns," likely referring to my seeming inability to follow his instructions properly. A pass was at least 75 points and I came up with, I think, something like 76 points. So, yes, it was passing by a whisker.

Was I relieved. And hoped that I would never have to take the driving exam from this character ever again. (As it turned out, I've never had to take the behind the wheel exam since that experience when I was sixteen years of age.)

Now, back to my vehicular life. (For a complete record of vehicles owned over the years, see Exhibit VI.)

So, my first automobile was that nice, two-door sky blue Pontiac Catalina with automatic transmission, with only three other automatics purchased since. I read somewhere recently that a few years back manual transmissions comprised about twenty percent of all cars on the road. Today, that figure has dropped to just one percent. Amazing. Manual transmissions are certainly a dying breed. In a few years I imagine non-autonomous cars will be included in the same category.

What was the first car I bought? That would be another Pontiac Catalina, a used 1962 model, and also sky blue in color. Also an automatic trans. I think I purchased that car around the year '65 or '66. In any case, it served me well during my college years at USF, and then at Berkeley. And I always associate that car with Vicky of Terra Linda since I have a picture of her standing next to it somewhere.

My next car was also used, a 1969 Chevrolet Camaro, dark blue in color with an automatic transmission, I believe. That was a great car as well.

After that, the first car that was brand spanking new was not a Pontiac or even a GM manufactured auto. It wasn't even American made. It was a 1973 Datsun 240Z, with a three-speed manual trans on the floor. It was gun metal gray with black leather interior.

I loved that car. It was the first that was actually fun to drive, probably because of its manual trans and all the associated shifting.

At this point my memory is beginning to elude me, but I believe my next vehicle was a 1979 Mazda RX7 with a rotary engine called a "Wankel." It was a beautiful metallic blue (I guess I had a thing about the color blue), with a manual trans; I believe it had four speeds forward.

I kept that car until 1987, when I purchased a used '86 Porsche 944T, (T" stands for "turbo") with only about 4,000 miles on it, and also with a manual trans. It was "Torch Red" in color, the same color as two other Porsches I would buy in the coming years. And it was also my first of up to five Porsches in total over the years. I really loved those Porsches.

When our family moved from Merced to Half Moon Bay in 1992, because of my new job at the San Mateo County Community College District, I traded down to a new Mazda Miata, the first of two I would buy. The Bay Area housing market was very expensive compared to Merced, with that being the reason I made that downward trade.

Once we were settled in and costs weren't quite as much of an issue, I traded the Miata in for a new 1996 Porsche 911, which was also Torch Red in color, again with a manual trans, perhaps with six speeds. (I'm not positive of that, however.)

Around the time of my separation and divorce, once again for cost considerations I traded down to a 1999 Mazda Miata; I believe it was green in color. That would be the last time I purchased a Miata.

After two or three years, and saving enough for a more expensive automobile, I traded the Miata in for a 2002 Audi TT Roadster. I recall it was silver in color with black leather interior. Also with a manual trans. I don't recall how many shifts on that floor mounted shifter though. That's all I can say at this point. My memory's going in the crapper.

Again, having made appropriate financial adjustments to my budget, I was able to purchase a new 2005 Porsche 911 Cabriolet, silver in color. But there was something just not right with that automobile, I don't recall what exactly. So, I turned around and traded it in the next year on a 2006 Porsche 911S, another Cabriolet, and black in color.

Now that was a great car, and I kept it until the year 2010. Again, going into retirement with reduced income, however, I decided to trade the Porsche for a less expensive Chevrolet Camaro, red in color, manual trans of course.

And a couple of years after that, I was going to trade the Camaro in for a convertible model in 2012, but there was a beautiful metallic blue Corvette on the same showroom floor that day. I immediately decided I wanted that Corvette, and negotiated a trade-in of the Camaro for that automobile.

That was one of my favorite cars. I had taken the Camaro to the drag strip in Sonoma and would eventually take the Corvette, with an aftermarket supercharger installed.

More on that adventure when I discuss my pastimes in an upcoming episode.

And as much as I loved that Corvette, a new Jaguar sports car had come out in 2014, called an "F-Type," and I decided to trade in the Corvette on it. The Jag was black in color with, I believe, an automatic transmission, one of the few I had. It was a beautiful car, but it wasn't a Porsche or a Corvette.

Wanting to return to the world of Porsches once again, and unable to afford a new 911, in the year 2016 I found one with only 4,000 miles of use on it back in the Midwest somewhere. It was a 2012 Torch Red Cabriolet model, practically identical to the '96 model I bought almost twenty years earlier. Same exterior and interior colors. Again, another manual trans. I had it hauled out in a covered trailer, and the seller took the trade of my Jaguar and loaded it into the same trailer to take back.

That was a great car as well, and I kept it until 2019, at which time I traded the Porsche in for a new 2019 convertible Corvette Z06, also red in color. With its seven speed manual trans, this particular auto already came with its own supercharger, with all of 650 horsepower, more than twice as much as that 1960 Pontiac that my brother and I took to the drag races almost sixty years earlier. To date I haven't had the pleasure of taking it drag racing, but I've read that it will go 134 mph in 10.6 seconds in the quarter mile. Another beast.

That poor Pontiac wouldn't have stood a chance, with its 90 mph, and accompanying 15.0 second elapsed time.

Such is the history behind the automobiles of C.T. Blake, all seventeen of them over the last fifty-eight years. At my age there will likely not be many more.

At least not until I get "the bug" for one more car to add to the list.

3 - About My Abodes

I've discussed the dwellings that my parents and I lived in over the years. Now, let's talk about those that I lived in as an adult.

Of course there were several dorms and other housing when I was a student at USF, UC Berkeley, and even UCLA. And there were some apartments when I started working. One of my personal favorites was a Spanish style four-plex on Prince Street in Oakland. It was a big roomy one bedroom (although it did have a big Murphy bed that folded out in the dining room of all places) which I had as a bachelor and that I shared with Elena when we first married. We occupied that apartment for only a brief period, however.

Then we purchased our very first home in Pinole. This was in 1975.

We had been doing a lot of searching prior to that purchase. Elena had lived in an El Cerrito apartment when I met her, and I in the Prince Street apartment. I had relatively high aspirations about our first home. Maybe a bit too high.

In the beginning of our search we concentrated on finding a house in the hills overlooking Berkeley, where both of us worked at the time. We also looked in Kensington, an enclave next to Berkeley. I was influenced by a friend, Mohan, who I worked with at the university. He and his wife had a home in Kensington at that time. They had built a large deck which had a magnificent view of the SF Bay Area. On one occasion we "house-sat" for them in that house and we absolutely fell in love with the ambiance of the hills.

As an aside, I will mention that Mohan and I had an ongoing debate as to which was better, a house with a deck view, or one with a swimming pool (in a home I would eventually buy).

Anyway, Mohan's area was a bit pricey for our limited means. The homes we looked at were usually over $60,000, which was quite a bit at the time. We both worked and could easily afford the payments that would accompany the purchase, but being first time home buyers we were a tad low on the necessary down-payment.

Realizing our dilemma we continued our search, but in the nearby hills of Albany and El Cerrito, where prices were more reasonable. There was one in El Cerrito, with a great view that we really liked. It was priced around $55,000, requiring down-payment and fees of $12,000. I think we scrapped together about $9,000 between the two of us.

We wanted to make an offer, but we needed that extra $3,000 to do so. I considered asking my parents for help. My dad was still working in his supermarket at the time and they didn't have a lot of expenses since they paid a low rent for the house behind the store. But I was afraid they would turn that loan into a gift, not expecting a repayment from us. And my dad was getting ready to retire within a few months and I wanted them to have the flexibility to buy that "house by the lake," which my dad dreamed of.

That's when we turned to another family member for help. That person was no "money-bags," but he was relatively frugal and had a history of loaning money to others to buy rental properties. And we knew there was no way he would forgive a loan to us. So, we would pay the $3,000 off over the next year.

Elena talked to him about the potential loan. I wasn't a party to that conversation, but Elena told me that he said the area we were looking at was a transitional area that we shouldn't consider. Therefore, no loan.

The area that home was in was far from transitional, and today those homes sell for upwards of $2 million. And the other folks he had lent money to, however, "invested" in properties in lower Richmond, which today sell for around $500 to 600 thousand.

"Transitional"? I don't think so.

So, with that option of a loan no longer available, we turned our attention to the Pinole area, where Elena's parents lived. It was about twelve miles from our workplace, but there were nice homes selling for less than $50,000 at that time. The one we could best afford was selling for $48,000. And we could have that home with our available funds plus a bit more that we threw together at the last minute.

The house was a rather small three bedroom, two bath affair, about 1300 square feet on a street with a neat name,

Shady Draw. (For complete record of residences see Exhibit V.)

Rather than think of that home as a "fallback option" because we couldn't afford the homes we really wanted, I try to relate it to the place where our first child, Matthew, was born, a positive memory.

Unfortunately, it has an associated bad memory since my father passed away shortly thereafter. I recall a picture of him, holding baby Matthew in his arms. I was glad that he at least had one grandchild to hold.

And soon we learned that another Blake baby, Jeffrey, would be arriving in the months ahead.

Realizing that the Shady Draw abode was a bit smallish for a family of four, and with the money we saved during the eighteen months we lived there, we traded up to a four bedroom home of 1,800 square feet on Simas Avenue, which was not far from Shady Draw. Our new home had a large back yard and a beautiful swimming pool. The hills behind the house and on its property had about forty stunning Redwood trees, adding to the allure.

The home was barely ten years old, so there wasn't much need for refurbishment with one exception. Our children were toddlers at the time and we had a concern about one or both of them falling into that nice big pool and drowning. So, we took care of that concern by erecting a tall wrought iron fence between the house and the pool. And we took great pains to ensure that the gate to the pool was always closed.

Matthew and Jeffrey eventually took swimming lessons to help alleviate our concern over a drowning. I recall that Jeff was a little less enthused about the swim lessons, but in due course he became a proficient swimmer along with his brother. In fact, years down the road when he was an adult, Jeff would buy a very nice motor boat with his family spending considerable time during summer on various lakes around the state.

With respect to that wonderful back yard, I recall in particular a memorable occasion involving the baptism of Jeffrey, when my college friend Guati came all the way from Hermosillo, Mexico, to serve as Jeff's Godfather. There were lots of folks there. We had a great time.

We spent ten years in that home, good years I think. The only negative during that time was an infestation of our Redwood trees, causing us to have them all chopped down. The once beautiful hillside was now barren. That was sad.

Next stop: Merced

When I took the job there, it was time to move again. After considerable searching in the town, we managed to find a brand new home in a very nice suburb of Merced.

The home was just built and looking for its first owner. It was located in a very attractive cul-de-sac on a street named "Santa Inez," with a more than adequate size lot. However, the single story house lacked a swimming pool. So, we had one built. We also had the contractor who built the house add a family room extension to the house. It already had what was called a "great room." But we wanted a separate family room.

The rest of the family, this time with Matthew and our second son, Jeffrey, stayed in Pinole until all the work was done. I lived in the house myself. When the work was complete and the boys were out of school, Elena, Matt and Jeff joined me in Merced.

During our time there, we considered buying other larger homes in the area, but remained in the Santa Inez home for the duration of my employment at the College.

That house had some good memories. The kids seemed to like their parochial school, St. Joseph's. And Elena and I particularly enjoyed the walks we could take along a large creek nearby.

However, when I landed the job in San Mateo, it was time to relocate once more. As I mentioned earlier, the SF Bay Area real estate was a bit much for our budget despite the fact I was making a good twenty thousand more a year. That was when a lady who was the president of Skyline College suggested we try out an area "over the hill" named Half Moon Bay (HMB).

I had always associated HMB with drag races since my brother took me to the drag strip in HMB many years ago. However, by 1992 it had taken on a new complexion, without a drag strip but with a nice enclave named Ocean Colony which was situated on a golf course. We had searched and searched on the other side of the hill and found nothing we could afford. I remember one home in Redwood City that I thought would be fine. Small. No pool. Older. The kids looked at it with disappointment all over their faces. That was the point where HMB started looking pretty good.

We looked at a couple of homes in Ocean Colony until we settled on one on a street named "Eagle Trace." The home was absolutely gigantic by our standards, about 3400 square feet, with five bedrooms, four baths plus bonus room. It didn't have a very large back yard, and there was no swimming pool, of course. Another disadvantage was its being adjacent to Highway 1. But there was a "sound wall" to muffle the noise of highway traffic and we all loved the house. We paid somewhere around $515,000 for this one.

We all liked the area, particularly for its golf course. I didn't play golf, but we could take long walks on the golf course trails which was nice. And sometimes the boys would sneak onto the course and play a few holes.

Sadly, the Eagle Trace residence would be the last abode that Elena and I shared.

Upon receiving dissolution papers, I moved into a small apartment in the hills of Burlingame, which I have already referred to. Shortly thereafter, I relocated from that apartment to another larger one in the same complex. This one had a deck with an expansive view of the SF Bay. It was great. I would sit out there at night taking in the view as I sipped some Chardonnay, not realizing that alcohol and drugs would soon become a major impediment in my life.

4 - The Redding Abode

I have discussed Redding elsewhere, but it's a place worth having its own episode in my life. Yes, and a very, very hot place at that.

Prior to moving from Half Moon Bay up to Redding, I always thought that Merced would be the hottest place we'd ever live in. However, the city of Redding takes the cake in terms of heat. The summer temperatures reach an average maximum of 99 degrees in the month of July, probably a couple of degrees higher than Merced would be at the same time of the year. And this year, the year 2021, the hot spell started a month early with temperatures reaching 114 degrees in the month of June.

Now, it would probably be unfair to relate this condition solely to our town with its 89,861 inhabitants. Temperatures soared everywhere in the northwest this summer season. Many surmise that this severe condition is the outcome of what is called "climate change." And the implication is that such changes are caused by humans burning fossil fuels which release carbon dioxide into the air.

So, we're not talking about a simple change in the weather; rather this climate change is something ongoing and is long-term. And we folks are the responsible party.

Enough lecturing on human frailty. Let's return to the topic of Redding itself. I moved here in 2013 by myself. Within about a year, my partner Rhonda retired from her job with the City of San Mateo and moved here as well. And as earlier mentioned, the two Ragamuffins made the trip northward. Also, as mentioned, I decided I needed an Akita friend, name of Zeus.

And some more felines entered the scene as well. One big, happy family.

But it didn't quite stop there. There is wildlife aplenty in our area west of the City of Redding. We've got squirrels, we've got deer, we've got turkeys; you name it, we've got it! I've even spotted a brown bear at least once.

And as if that was not enough, I "adopted" a donkey named "Billy" down the road who I occasionally visit, giving him a brushing when I do. Sometimes he also gets some celery or some carrots, although we try to stay away from those food stuffs that are not good for donkeys, particularly for this guy who has a history of leg problems. After all, he's probably going on forty years at this point.

I don't visit him as much this summer because of the heat, but I should since he's not going to be around forever. I'll try to do better.

As to our immediate abode on Texas Springs Road, I thought the Eagle Trace home would be the largest I'd ever live in until I got here with the $575,000 property that Rhonda and I bought together.

Our new home has four bedrooms with one used as an office at present.

Downstairs we have a large living room, a nice dining room, and the room with the piano and books that we call the "culture room." The master bedroom and attached bath is also located downstairs which is convenient. There are two other half-baths on the first floor.

And there's never a problem with the availability of a toilet as we have five of those spread around the two floors.

We're in the process of refurbishing the living room with new carpet, circular in nature, and new set composed of sofa, love seat and rocker-recliner chair.

Upstairs we have the office, two guest bedrooms, two full bathrooms, and a bonus room which houses around 1,400 books. We now refer to this room as our "library."

Unlike the Eagle Trace home, this one has air conditioning which we obviously need during the hot Redding summers, several overhead fans, as well as a "master cooler" which is sufficient when temperatures are at a more manageable level (no more than 90 degrees outside).

All told, we have about 3,550 square feet of living space the last time I checked on that statistic.

There is a very large three car garage with work bench and an area for our generator.

Whereas the Eagle Trace property was on a relatively small lot, this one sits on about three acres, plus or minus. With so many trees of all descriptions surrounding our home, that I've lost count (I'd hazard a guess of about two hundred of those guys).

We're fortunate to employ a gardening crew that comes in weekly.

Unlike the Eagle Trace home, this one has its own fully enclosed swimming pool and a large separate enclosed yard where Zeus can run like crazy.

It's worth noting that every summer Rhonda and I talk about moving to some place like Oregon or Washington to escape the heat. We talk about that a lot, but do nothing; I'm guessing we'll be here forever (whatever "forever" means in our case).

External to our home there is enough "culture" in the town if we wish to take advantage of it. I don't know if it's culture or not, but we've seen Boz Skaggs a couple of times plus some other groups like the Four Tops. And there's even more culture that we don't necessarily take advantage of.

Things like car shows called "Kool April Nights." Although because of the COVID, that did not take place last year, and this time around it was down-scaled to something called the "Show and Shine."

Perhaps the biggest attraction, at least from my point of

view, is something not even in Redding; that's Whiskeytown Lake about ten miles away where I've gone sailing when I had a sailboat. More on that adventure in an upcoming episode about my life of leisure.

We mostly have nice neighbors nearby, although several of them relocated last year to places like Las Vegas, Nevada, and Billings, Montana. Their replacements are mostly okay, but we don't really socialize with them so it's kind of hard to tell.

I think that pretty much covers our Redding abode.

5 - If One is Good, Two are Better

Time for a change in subject, a very serious subject.

Some folks have what is called an addictive personality. Although one tends to think of alcohol and drugs, there are many types of addictions; one with that personality just can't seem to say no (despite Nancy Reagan's "Just Say No" advice) to whatever it is that they are consumed with.

Although I always suspected I may have such a personality, I didn't begin to fully recognize it until alcohol took such a grip on me around the time of the new millennium.

Oftentimes, there is an underlying cause to prompt the addictive personality into "action." In my case, it could have been the separation and divorce. Or it could have been work-related. Or a combination of the two. Whatever it was, it took over. And only alcohol would seem to relieve it

Not only did I drink excessively, but I also drank at the most inappropriate times. I would literally push the envelope of addiction that had a hold on me. I drank at home, sometimes even in the morning. I drank prior to driving. I even went into work on some weekends with a hangover from the prior night.

I was surprised that others did not notice my condition when I had been drinking, or was hang-over. Or maybe they did, but just kept their mouths shut.

There are good ways and bad ways to deal with an alcohol or drug addiction. Some find that a twelve-step program works for them. I very briefly tried that approach, but it didn't work for me.

Others try some form of counseling. I tried that as well. But by itself, that didn't work for me either. And I tried quite a few counselors in the process. Some were local. One was on Van Ness Avenue in San Francisco. And they weren't cheap either.

Finally, I thought I had found something that would work for me. I was fooling myself, however, when one day I ran across an old prescription for the painkiller, Vicodin, in the medicine cabinet. I don't recall exactly what it had been prescribed for. I took a couple of those opiates. Wow, did that ever feel good! Not just good, but great! I soon developed a fondness for the drug. So much so that I realized my medicine cabinet supply would run out.

I needed a steady and reliable source. And that's when I learned that you could go online and order hoards of the stuff. Not cheap, but doable. And there was more than one source for my choice of opiate. I don't think that the Fentanyl opiate was available at the time. And given the nature of that opiate, I was likely very lucky.

I was also experiencing sleep problems. That's when I learned that I could get sleeping aids as well as pain killers online. There my drug of choice was Ambien. So I now had a "partner" of sorts to go along with my Vicodin friend.

Once again, life was just great. But, as I said, I was fooling myself.

The problem with opiates is a little different from alcohol. They both can be problematic; however, in the case of opiates, if one is good, two is better. And if two are better, than three or four are better yet. And so it goes.

As it turns out, unlike alcohol, you begin to develop a tolerance for the opiate causing you to need more of it to achieve the same effect.

It got to the point where I was taking up to twenty of those tablets every day. Now it was totally out of hand.

I remember a trip we took to Maui. As we were walking down the promenade, I pulled out a few of the tablets, hoping that no one saw me, and took them without even having water to wash them down. That's how bad it was at that point.

It's hard to say how long this went on since I was operating in a fog, a fog of inebriation. However long it was, it was too long. I couldn't continue to load myself up with a drug that dulls the senses to this degree and ultimately not have a major problem.

There was likely a turning point, but I can't remember when or what that turning point was. And I can't quite remember how

I came to this conclusion. What I do recall is that once I had a counselor who was also a psychiatrist who could prescribe medicine, I slowly began to turn the corner on my opiate world.

I think of the medication I was prescribed as a "miracle drug." Others would say it's just another addiction, a crutch. In any event, it worked and that's what was most important.

Shortly thereafter I found a medical practice in South San Francisco that specialized in addiction. There was more than one doctor in that practice.

I would ultimately rotate through all of them as each one retired from their practice.

The drug I refer to as a miracle, is called Suboxone. I don't completely understand its properties, but through its use, the craving for opiates is relieved to the extent that one can return to a state of "normality" in daily life.

Surprisingly, I have now been on this medication for almost twenty years. And during that time I have had no craving at all for opiates, or for that matter, alcohol. I can now function as a real, live human being. And for that I am quite thankful.

I regularly see my current physician every three months. Those visits are required for him to prescribe the Suboxone. While there is no counseling going on when I see my doctor, he still addresses anything related to the medication during our sessions. And sometimes I get a "freebie" in terms of advice related to other matters involving my physical being.

There is a side benefit to my doctor visits since it gives me an opportunity to get out of the house and drive my Corvette the two hundred and forty miles necessary to get to his Burlingame office.

It doesn't get driven enough so this is great.

I don't know how long I will continue to see my physician, or how long I will continue to take this medication, but probably until the end of my life whenever that is.

But that's okay, because I'm back to "normal."

6 - Life of Leisure

I've already begun to address my life of leisure by noting my change in residences since retiring. However, I didn't cover what I've done with this life. Actually, that's quite a bit. And I don't really know exactly where to start because there's so much to talk about.

Of course, there are some pastimes that I took up earlier in my life but have not as yet pursued. One example is scuba diving. I took up this sport after Sally left for southern California and I was lonely. I went through a local dive shop in Berkeley, and bought the required diving stuff I'd need.

They also offered lessons. I took the basic course and, upon completion, I then took a more advanced course. During those lessons, both beginning and advanced, we would go to places like Mendocino and Monterey to experience all that you can when you're anywhere from twenty to more than one hundred feet below the surface.

I did some diving on my own (but always with a dive buddy as recommended) including a couple of dives in Hawaii. That's a place that you really want to have the diving opportunity.

What you can witness at the hundred foot plus depth I went to in Hawaii is unbelievable. I wish I could go back. Maybe I will someday. Probably unlikely at my age, however. But at least I have the memories (as well as some pictures I took at depth).

There are also pursuits from the past that I've returned to once again. One example would be sailing, which I took up around the time that Sally left for southern California, the same time I took up scuba diving. The two seemed to go together well.

My first experiences with sailing were on the San Francisco Bay when I took lessons offered by the Cal sailing club. Those lessons were on sailboats called "Ensigns," boats about twenty-three feet in length.

Once I learned to sail, I would try it in venues beyond SF Bay. I recall one experience when a friend of mine, Kevin, and I drove up to Lake Tahoe. When we were there, we rented a small sailboat called a "Laser" which is really designed for one person, not two.

In any case, I remember that "adventure" clearly. Kevin wasn't familiar with sailboats and how to operate them, so I was trying to give him some little lessons as we sailed out on the Lake about a half-mile or so.

I was in the process of teaching him about "heeling" the boat (which causes the boat to tip to one side), and had given him the sheet (the rope) to pull back on which tightened up the sail and causes the Laser to move faster, which it did. If you've ever done this with a Laser, you can imagine it tipping to one side and speeding onward.

It seems fast when you're on it, but you really can't go more than ten to twelve knots (I read that the record is a bit over 13). So, here we are heeling away and picking up speed when I accidentally slip off the side of the boat, going into the drink. Fortunately, we had life jackets on. Nonetheless, there I was in the middle of the Lake with Kevin continuing to pull tight on the rope, moving farther away from me.

I yelled at him to drop the rope, but he didn't seem to hear me until the point that he realized I was gone and had a look of terror on his face, finally dropping the rope. Since he knew nothing about how to get back to me, I ended up having to swim what seemed like a mile, but was actually more like fifty yards, back to Kevin and the sailboat. I'm a fairly decent swimmer but I have to admit, that little swim was a bit scary. If I got a cramp or something else, I would have been in big trouble.

I think at that point we decided to call it a day and headed back to shore.

I wonder if good old Kevin remembers that experience?

I never had my own sailboat, only rentals. So, retirement was now an opportunity to change that. I surveyed the field and finally decided that a brand new twenty-seven foot sailboat, called a MacGregor (ironically that was the nickname Rhonda had already assigned to me, sometimes calling me Craigor or Astro MacGregor), along with a trailer and outboard engine, was affordable.

I drove up to the Seattle area where there was an exhibition of boats of all kinds, including that MacGregor. I fell in love with it, almost as much as some of the cars I've bought. Had to have it. So, it was purchased with the understanding that the company I bought it from would deliver it to our nearby Whiskeytown Lake, a perfect place for sailing.

That was a couple of years ago. It was fun. I took it out on the lake several times. Usually alone. I admit it was a challenge for me without a "first mate." But I could handle it until one day when I took a kayak out to where the boat was moored. As I was standing on the kayak and trying to pull myself up into the boat, I slipped and fell into the water. Fortunately, I again had a life jacket on. As much as I tried, for the life of me I couldn't get back on that kayak, let alone the boat itself. Finally, a couple in another kayak came along and I was able hitch a ride with them as they "towed" me all the way back to shore.

That was the last time I stood up on a kayak.

I continued to enjoy sailing through the summer and into the fall. But there was something about leaving that sailboat anchored in the water by itself that bothered me. It felt almost like leaving a baby in a stroller somewhere and walking off. I would go out more than once to check on it even when I wasn't going to sail.

After about one year, I decided that I probably wasn't going to get the use out of it that I initially planned on. So I put it up for sale and found a buyer from southern California. With his purchase, I managed to get back about eighty percent of what I had paid for it. As to the twenty percent difference, that's probably pretty close to what it would have cost me to rent a sailboat during the period I owned one.

And so that was the end of my sailing life on Whiskeytown Lake.

Of course, I can always rent a boat if I want the experience that goes with sailing. However, for now at least, I can check off one more leisure interest on my "bucket list."

7 - Life's a Drag (Race)

In the twilight of my years, around the age of sixty-five, I decided that I should experience drag racing. So I took my car, which at that point was a Chevrolet Camaro, to the drag strip.

I really never had any experience in racing cars, drag racing or otherwise, unlike my brother who frequented drag strips, with one notable exception: when I was about fourteen years of age, my brother and I invested $400 in a little Go-Kart with a 2.5 hp Clinton engine, which we took to a racing track. I think it was in Petaluma.

I recall that at this race track, they gave you some practice laps in your Go-Kart before the actual races.

The races themselves were organized by engine size and horsepower. Of course, I was in the entry level group with my small 2.5 hp Clinton. I recall I was pretty nervous when the flag went down and I took off with all the other karts. If my memory serves me correctly, the race lasted about five laps.

And was I surprised when I somehow managed to come in second place in my first (and last as it turned out) race in that little Go-Kart! Boy, was I ever happy about that. I savored the moment.

As with my first car, I would eventually become very popular with that Go-Kart. I recall some high school friends coming over to our Santa Venetia residence one Saturday to take turns riding it. I remember one guy, Rich, drove over in his Corvette which he let me drive while he was having fun of his own on that Go-Kart. It was a great trade!

So, back to drag racing. Again, races were organized by engine size at the Sonoma track. I was probably more nervous the first time than in my Go-Kart race experience. The first car I ran against was burning rubber like crazy prior to the flag going down. And when it did, we both took off down the quarter mile track. I did okay, but I didn't win. As a matter of fact, I lost more often than I won in those matchups. But that was okay; I was having more fun than I had in quite some time. I think my best race that day clocked me at 104 miles per hour at the finish with an elapsed time of 13.3 seconds.

I thought that it might be even more fun if I had some company so after that first experience I invited various folks to go with me to the track. There was the father of my daughter-in-law Loree. His name is the same as my son's. Jeff. A real nice guy. I also took a friend from my San Mateo CCCD days, whose name was Darwin.

And, of course, I ultimately took my brother Reid after we had our reunion. That was very enjoyable as I kind of "reciprocated" with that event similar to the times that he took me to the drag races when he raced his Pontiac over fifty years ago.

I returned to the drag strip with my next car, a 2014 Corvette. I had installed an aftermarket supercharger in it which raised its horsepower from 425 to over 600. I wrongly assumed it would easily beat the Camaro's efforts. Although it went 113 mph at the end of the quarter mile, I couldn't improve on the 13.3 second ET. That super charged Corvette was a beast and even with special racing tires, I had major traction problems as the rear wheels spun round and round, probably chewing up more than a second of ET right at the outset. Clearly, I needed to "upgrade" my drag racing skill set.

What other retirement pastimes are on my bucket list?

Many years ago when my father was still alive, he would collect coins that came through his store. When he passed away, I inherited his collection. In the beginning, almost fifty years ago, I didn't do much of anything with that collection. However, that changed with retirement when I began to add to it. Mostly, I focused on "Morgan's." Those are silver dollars minted anywhere from 1878 through 1921. I'm now at the point that I have collected all of those from the various mints, San Francisco, New Orleans, Carson City, to have a complete collection.

I also have an almost complete collection of Peace dollars. Those range from 1921 through 1935. I continue to work on those.

And then there are the half-dollars including Franklins, Walking Liberties, and Kennedys. I've got a lot of those three.

There are also the more recent American Silver Eagle dollars, originally starting in 1986 and continuing on through today. And add to that the Eisenhower and presidential dollars that I've collected. You name it, I've got them.

I keep all the coins in albums of various sizes. In addition to the silver dollars and half-dollars noted above, I keep pennies, nickels, dimes and quarters in small albums.

While I have some coins that are in not-such-great condition, I try to acquire coins that are of a decent grade. Numismatists, those who study and/or collect coins, usually have their coins "graded." Based on the coin's various attributes, the grading has levels ranging from the lowest grade, AG (meaning "About Good") all the way up to the MS grade (which means "Mint State") where there are multiple levels.

I try to stay away from coins any lower than AU, meaning "About Uncirculated" grade (from AU-50 to AU 58). Unless the coins are unreasonably expensive, I shoot for the MS grade (which can range from MS-60 to MS-70).

Most of my acquisitions are purchased from various companies, although I've found a few in banks such as the Bank of America. One company in particular that has been fruitful is called APMEX. And they have a Web site on which you can actually maintain an inventory of sorts.

Recently, I had a bad experience with my collection. I maintain a fairly detailed spreadsheet of my monthly budget of both income and expenditures. (After all, in one of my "other lives" I was a budget director.) My budget projects out at least two years.

Unfortunately, I wasn't watching my monthly budget as closely as I should have, what with all my new pastimes. And because of an error in my expenditure budget, I ended up "overbuying" coins.

That put me into debt by a couple of thousand dollars, which took a while to recapture.

I'll pay more attention to that budget from here on out.

8 - A Bit of Culture

Other retirement pursuits?

Those would be astronomy, learning piano, and writing novels.

With respect to astronomy, I started with a small four inch aperture Celestron telescope until I decided to trade up to a larger eight inch one. It's fairly sophisticated, allowing one to program it so that it automatically locates whatever planets or star systems you're interested in. I readily admit that I haven't even scratched the surface in terms of being able to utilize its many capabilities.

I clearly need to do some more reading of the literature that came with the scope.

While I enjoy looking at the nighttime sky, at this stage of my life, my two "passions" are learning piano and writing. More on piano a little later. Regarding my writings, this memoir is one example, but I've also written and self-published three novels.

How did I get into this particular pursuit? It all started with a change in my reading activity.

At one time I read non-fiction books almost entirely. That was until my partner Rhonda convinced me some time back that there were rewards associated with reading fiction. So, I shifted my habits from non-fiction to almost entirely fiction.

One of our rooms downstairs, designated as the "culture room," houses some of our books but also a Yamaha baby grand piano. However, that room got so loaded with books that we had no place for the remaining 1,400 books we'd acquired.

At that point we knew what we had to do with an empty bonus room of about three hundred square feet upstairs. So, we purchased twenty small bookcases (since the vertical aspect of the walls only go up about four feet), and put them in the bonus room to house all the books we had beyond those that were already downstairs in the culture room.

Note that the culture room was formerly referred to as our "library," but when we decided to move our baby grand piano from its living room location to the library, the room took on a new theme, and that's when we started referring to it as the culture room.

Somewhere along the way, I decided that in addition to reading novels, maybe I should write one. That resulted in the story, *In Search of Sarah: A Time Traveler's Quandary*, which I wrote in the year 2015. And, after that, two more.

What is the *Sarah* story all about? Actually, it's pretty autobiographical, involving an older male named Scott McGregor, who reflects on an incident fifty years earlier in which he helped his girlfriend (name of Sarah, of course) in going to Mexico to procure an abortion of the fetus they are jointly responsible for.

I was never under the illusion that my novel could be published through a mainstream publisher. Maybe I could make that happen, but it would involve a lot of time and energy. First, finding an agent to represent me and then having the agent identify a publisher.

Recently I read about a lady, actually an airline flight attendant, who wrote a pretty good "debut" novel, but had to go through something like forty-two agents before finding one who liked her work enough to get her book published.

I don't think I have that kind of energy, assuming I had a book that was publishable in the first place.

So, in such a situation, what does one do?

You go and pay a "self-publishing firm," of which there are quite a few, to take over your project. That can cost as little as $800 on up to several thousand depending upon what kind of end product you'd like.

If you're willing to take on the costs involved, you can have your novel printed and available through Web sites such as Amazon or Barnes and Noble.

At the present, I have gone through this process three times, all with the same firm. I've probably spent at least four thousand dollars on getting my three novels printed and available to audiences. More on this later.

However, if you want to generate sales of your book, you also need to get reviews on the same Web sites. This can be time consuming, and sometimes humiliating, as you almost have to beg, borrow and steal for such reviews.

I'm partial, of course, but I think *Sarah's* a pretty good story, particularly with the time traveling component. I'm a time travel addict myself, and I love those kind of stories and films. So, coupled with my own experience with real life Sally, and my time travel interests, it was a natural outgrowth.

So, after writing it, I decided it should have a sequel in which Scott McGregor's son Jeff, and his partner's daughter Mackenzie, would play the main characters.

However, I had wrongly assumed that once I got my first novel on Amazon, the books would begin to fly off the Amazon shelves. Why did I think this? I saw what I considered to be some fairly lame novels getting a hundred or more reviews, so I set a goal of getting two hundred.

Was I in for a big surprise! I got nowhere near those two hundred. Nowhere near one hundred reviews. What did I get? A paltry six.

That's when the hard reality of the Amazon experience sunk in. I did some research on this matter, only to realize that the Web site got something like tens of thousands of new titles every year, most of which were buried in the wasteland of Amazon.

Where would my novel turn up in this wasteland? Well, at that time, the year 2015, I typed in the key subjects in my first novel such as, "time travel," "abortion," "Mexico," "Juarez," and the name "Sarah," with my title not turning up anywhere in the twenty-some iterations of the search, amounting to something like five hundred or so novels.

The novel only appeared when I entered the first part of the title, *In Search of Sarah*.

Conclusion: the only copies that would be sold would be those wherein the potential buyer was actually looking for my novel.

No one was going to stumble on it, that was for sure.

So, after the disappointing results with *Sarah*, I lost interest in pursuing more "literary efforts."

It took another five years before I worked up the energy and the courage, to return to my HP Pavilion and start banging out another novel entitled, *Dark Matters: In Search of Mackenzie*. I managed to whip that guy out in record time, about three months. And then went with the same self-publishing firm to get it into print and availability on Amazon.

And I didn't stop there. I quickly banged out a successor novel to *Dark Matters*, called *Dark Futures*. Again, it took only about three months to finish the sequel to the sequel, and get it out as well.

At that point, I was on a roll, and decided that another *Dark* novel should be written. The first novel involved time travel. The second involved travel to other dimensions. And the last of the three involved both concepts. So this fourth time around, I thought I'd take a swing at extraterrestrials arriving at Jeff's doorstep, with the appropriate title, *Dark Arrivals.*

But I began to feel torn over whether I really had the requisite energy for one more. After about twenty pages, I began to lose interest in the project. At around the same time, I communicated with an old school friend named Jim. He was telling me about his ongoing experience writing about his life. I hadn't given much thought to it, but that inspired me to switch my focus from a novel this time to a memoir. That was the point in time when this work had its genesis.

I didn't begin this project with the notion that it would be a best seller. Who would want a story about a neophyte author who sold very few books to begin with? The driving factor for this particular effort was for me to see my life experiences in printed form and maybe for my sons and a few others to read about it.

Now regarding those two "*Dark*" novels, I hadn't gone on the publisher's Web site since I had published them over the past year; I wasn't motivated to do that and see the same disappointing results as with *Sarah*.

But then I got another surprise of a quite different nature a few days ago when I received a nice royalty check in the mail. And along with it a list of the sales dates. I then went on what is called the "Author Login" of my publisher to see the exact number of those novels that brought up that nice royalty check.

It turned out that the sales of both *Dark Matters* and *Dark Futures* over the past three or four months far exceeded those of my earlier effort.

I also learned that if I simply typed in my name, "Craig Blake," Amazon would bring up all three of my novels in the very first round.

I'm not sure why. Perhaps the Amazon algorithm has been improved since 2015? Or maybe those extra sales pushed my books higher up in the cue?

Who knows?

In any case, I was now back in business with a renewed enthusiasm for continuing writing beyond this memoir.

9 - Five Easy Pieces

In addition to writing, my other passion is learning to play the piano.

I should have started this long ago when Rhonda and I saw a Yamaha baby grand piano in Costco in May of 2008, and given my covetous nature, decided I needed that piano. At that time I wasn't sure I would actually learn to play; however, this particular piano was an electronic self-playing type of piano called a Disklavier.

So, my logic went, even if I don't actually learn to play it, at least I can listen to the piano music I love so much on the Disklavier. Since then I have purchased over eighty Disklavier discs which I listen to from time to time.

However, sometime around March, 2016, some eight years after the purchase of my Disklavier, I finally made a decision: one way or another I was going to learn to play.

I didn't want to take lessons from a teacher; I was pretty sure that wouldn't work given my "independent" nature (so well expressed years earlier by my friend Ted). I would do it on my own, and that's when the "adventure" began.

It is now more than five years since then and I'm still going at it. Some weeks I put in more time than others. And when I'm off on my companion adventure of writing, I spend a bit less time with the piano.

In the early going, for about three or four years, I kept detailed records of when I played, which tunes, and the amount of time weekly that I devoted to the effort. However, I found I was spending too much time on record keeping and not enough time on actual practice. So, I stopped the record keeping some time back.

But I still manage to devote a few hours weekly to the effort.

Over time, I've found that some genres appeal to me more than others. Mostly I enjoy listening to and learning jazz-oriented music, particularly those with their origins going back to the thirties, forties and fifties.

Some examples of pieces I particularly enjoy are as follows: "April in Paris," "As Time Goes By," Bewitched," "Body and Soul," "Fly Me to the Moon," "I Left My Heart in San Francisco," "I'll Be Seeing You," "I'll Remember April," "Indiana," "Isn't It Romantic?," "Mood Indigo," "Night and Day," "'Round Midnight," and "What's New?"

I have Disklavier disks for many of these pieces, which I can play to get a better sense of how they should sound. This can also be a rude awakening for me if I'm doing a poor job on the ivories. I have tried to record what I play on a little recording device, but

I don't like what I hear. Not sure it's due to the device itself or my playing.

If I don't have the corresponding disks for pieces I play, then I turn to CD music which the electronics of the piano can also play. Sometimes I have both.

While I no longer keep the daily record of my learning process, I continue to maintain an inventory of each and every Disklavier piece, by source and pianist when available. And I maintain a similar inventory for the non-Disklavier music that I have.

In terms of where I find my sheet music, they come from multiple sources. One of the better on-line sources is called musicnotes.com, and those probably comprise eighty percent of all of my sheet music. I also keep an inventory of my printed sheet music.

In terms of how I learn, my approach is probably not the approach that most pianists and/or teachers would recommend. My "process" involves first identifying music that sounds not only interesting, but also seems like something I could learn. And then I print out the sheet music.

So, here's the part which teachers would probably not advise. I actually write the names of the notes next to the notes, e.g., next to the note "E", I write "E." And where there are two or more notes together such as "E" and "G", I write that over the notes themselves. As I have already indicated, this approach is likely not recommended by professional piano people; however, it works quite well for me.

The problem with this approach is that if I ever decide not to rely on it, it will be extremely difficult to "relearn" the notes by looking only at the lines they are on.

So, I speculate that I probably will never veer from this approach of learning music.

After several years of practice, I find that my fingers do seem to go to where they need to be automatically without consciously thinking of where they should be, as when I was first learning.

Unfortunately, I am still not at a point where I can play a piece by memory without the related sheet music.

Maybe someday. Not today.

In the meanwhile, I will continue things as they are. And while I have almost one hundred pieces I concentrate on and can regularly play, I have hundreds of possible pieces to choose from for further practice. That could keep me quite busy for a long time into the future.

What I like about my piano practice is that it's a nice complement to my writing. Both are quite good learning adventures. Sometimes when I'm tired of writing, I go to my piano. And sometimes when I'm finished with piano, I turn to writing.

Oftentimes, when I'm tired of writing, I go downstairs to our so-called culture room where the 5 foot, 3 inch baby grand resides, and then practice for 30 minutes or so. It's quite refreshing.

And I do have "Five Easy Pieces" that are not really easy, but I like to focus on: "Like Someone in Love," "Lullaby of Birdland," "Midnight Sun," "My Foolish Heart," and "Spring is Here."

I don't think I'll ever tire of playing piano.

10 - Passions Unrealized

I've discussed writing and piano as two of my passions. I could easily refer to them as "passions realized." I recognize their existence as components of my life from which I derive pleasure. In so doing, however, I must also ask myself: Are there other potential pastimes from which I could derive pleasure but have yet to explore?

I know what at least one of them could be: drawing and/or painting.

Way back when I referred to a few incidents related to this subject. In one case early on in my grammar school years a couple of the "terror" students asked me if I could draw a naked lady. I probably could have but avoided doing it by saying I had to pee.

The other incidents involved the mother of one of my classmates who asked me to develop posters for an upcoming event. Around the same time, one of my classmates running for class president recognized my artistic skill by asking me to be his campaign manager (ostensibly so that I could do his posters).

At the risk of sounding vain, in each of these situations my inherent artistic abilities were recognized. But for whatever reason I've never pursued that talent beyond some sketching I did of horses when I was young. I really loved those horses.

Similar to my inspiration for writing a memoir, I had another one recently. And it also relates to the writings of one of my favorite authors, Stephen King. A conversation with my friend Jim got me thinking about the subject. However, it was King's book, *On Writing*, that provided me with a kind of template for how to go about the effort.

This came about as I was reading one of his past novels, *Duma Key*, the other night. The novel involves a character named Edgar Freemantle. I digress a bit here. Freemantle is a contractor who has a horrific accident which results in multiple injuries to his eyes, his legs, and the very worst requiring the amputation of one of his arms.

As a result of these injuries, he consults with several specialists including a psychiatrist named Kamen. Kamen knows Freemantle's history in contracting, a history that precluded his taking time from work to enjoy any kind of outside activity. So Kamen asks him what he would enjoy doing if he had the time (which, of course, he now has plenty of). Freemantle tells him that when he was young he always enjoyed "sketching."

So, Kamen tells him to do two things: First, "Go on a geographical." In other words, go to another part of the country, and when he gets there he should take up the second thing, pursuing his enjoyment of sketching. And maybe even painting.

Freemantle ends up moving to an island off the west coast of Florida called Duma Key (which is a fictional locale near Sarasota, coincidentally where King himself spends some of his time when he's not in his native New England). And that idyllic island constitutes the perfect place for him to return to his love of drawing.

Freemantle is quite surprised when others, including an art gallery owner, upon seeing his work, believe he has a great talent ready to be harnessed.

So, this was my inspiration to "go beyond the horses." Maybe it's time to take up drawing and possibly painting with acrylics or oils.

I could pursue that activity by taking a course at the local community college; however, the lingering threat of the so-called "Delta variant" causes me to avoid such an environment at this time.

So, I went to the Amazon Web site and ordered some books on the subjects of drawing and painting. And if I like what I read and what I see, I may just go to an arts and crafts store and get an easel, some sketchpads, and the appropriate drawing instruments to begin yet another new adventure.

That's what I'll do.

11 - Friends Along the Way

By the time one reaches my age, one becomes more reflective on life, and death, which is a frequent visitor, as well. And at this age, one has probably met ninety percent or more of all the people that one could know. That's just a wild ass guess I pulled out of the air, but it makes sense to me.

Along with that recognition, one also begins to witness friends and relatives alike who pass away. Most prominent among those, in my case, is my brother Reid who passed away just a few years ago. I had only been in contact with him for around five years after our reunion when he rather abruptly passed away. And now I will miss him. In recognition of him and his effect on my life, I dedicated my last book, *Dark Futures*, to his memory.

More recently, I was saddened to learn of the death of my cousin CeCe. While I had not seen her in years, more recently we maintained ongoing contact through email almost weekly. So, with her passing there's now another big void in my life. I miss her and I miss our communications very much. In recognition of that now broken connection, I dedicated my earlier novel, *Dark Matters*, to her memory.

Such dedications have more irony related to the titles of those books. It's a kind of darker future without my brother around. And when CeCe died suddenly last year, it certainly was a kind of dark matter.

Years ago, I dedicated that first novel, *In Search of Sarah*, to Sally who I had not seen or been in contact with for more than forty years. I still felt a connection with her for whatever reason and that was the genesis of that novel which is autobiographical with its story and which parallels our relationship at that time in our lives.

This time around, I am dedicating these memoirs to my parents, Reinhart and Grace Blake, who I probably should have dedicated in a novel long before this. However, they passed away forty-one and twenty-eight years ago, respectively. And as such, the loss associated with their passing had its impact long ago. But their memories continue on.

I continue to maintain contact with others, both friends and relatives, largely through the vehicle of electronic mail, a form of communication which has been in existence for a good thirty-plus years now. While it doesn't have the intimacy of physical contact or even telephone communication, it's readily available and does provide more than adequate linkage with those afar.

One example of that linkage is the one with my former Merced College secretary, Dee, who I worked with over thirty years ago.

Sometimes the contact with her involves merely jokes she

sends me; other times its news about her family and the friends we shared years ago. And that connection will likely continue until that time when one of us "parts the scene."

There are other connections from the Merced College era. One is Susan, the College librarian at the time I was the VP of administrative services. Contact with her has been a little more erratic for all kinds of reasons. For example, recently I asked for her advice on a matter relating to her field of library research. And there was some back-and-forth on that matter.

Unfortunately, her partner recently passed away, at which time I once again reached out to her to offer my sincere condolences. That type of situation makes me more aware of our limited time on the planet and why that means we should continue to revisit the folks from the past from time to time as we never know when that connection may be broken forever.

And there are others who we may not have been real close to over the years, but always enjoyed seeing when the opportunity presented itself. A good example of that is my son's mother-in-law, Linda, who recently passed away due to an ongoing illness. I didn't see her all that often, but I always enjoyed our meetings when the occasion arose. And I had an association with her husband, Jeff, over the years. As I mentioned earlier, he too was a drag race friend who joined me at the Sonoma drag strip in the past.

In my writings, I have referred to my friend and college roommate, Guati, more than once. He is also my son Jeff's Godfather. I miss seeing him in person; it's been years since our last meeting but that's okay as we continue to go the email route. He's been a loyal friend and helpmate; recently he was good enough to not only order my book (as I've said, very few have), but also to buy an additional copy for a friend of his.

Those are the kind of little things about a person that can make all the difference in the case of long distance relationships.

And there are those friends from the past that we have been out of touch with until one day when contact is initiated once more. This occurred when I recently sent out some post cards advertising my latest novel, *Dark Futures*. In response to his receipt of one of those post cards, I was pleasantly surprised to receive an email from my friend Jim, who I knew throughout much of our education, elementary and high school, and then briefly in college at USF. I had not heard from Jim in many years.

With his contact, we were able to renew acquaintances and update each other on our lives since college, which was great. It was a challenging contact for us, however, since Jim is legally blind and cannot easily read emails. He suggested phone contact and I had to tell him I've got a hearing disability, making that mode not easy for me!

We compromised with my sending him emails with an 18 size font.

When he heard about my novels, Jim was interested in reading them, but his disability was a limiting factor in that regard. However, he was good enough to pull up an audible version which he could listen to.

In my communications with Jim, I learned that despite his sight limitations, he oftentimes would write about his various experiences in the past. That was actually the main impetus for this effort as I noted in the prologue. It really got me thinking about my life and how much of it I wanted to share with others, particularly my sons.

I just hope they read it once it's available to them. Maybe it will make a difference in their lives.

12 - About Our Sons

Speaking of my sons (at the end of the last episode), and before I talk about the future, I really need to talk about Matthew and Jeffrey.

Some of their history has been addressed sporadically in prior episodes. But that doesn't do them justice.

To recount a bit: Matt was born in March of 1976, when Elena and I lived in the memorable Shady Draw home in Pinole. Jeff arrived on the scene shortly thereafter, in June of 1977, when we were at the Simas address just a few blocks away.

And each of them has been very successful in his own right since then.

However, prior to discussing them and their successes, an anecdote or two, starting with Matt. I recall the day he was born quite clearly. I may not have been completely ready and able for that occasion since it was Elena's and my first baby.

It all started the night before when Elena told me, "It's time to go."

So how did I react to that piece of news? I'm sure that Elena remembers it as well as I do. I took a shower and got dressed in my best pre-birth clothes.

This is somewhat akin to what happened when my mother was near death and I decided I needed to go to work to take care of some things before I went to see her that fateful day. However, that situation was no laughing matter, but I think this one bordered on comical.

Taking a shower? Why did I need to take an extra twenty minutes or so when Elena was ready to do what expectant mothers do in that situation? I think Elena was beside herself when she heard the shower running and realized I didn't seem to be reacting the way a husband should be reacting.

However, there was a reason for that particular behavior and it was prescient to some degree. When she inquired as to why I was taking a shower and picking out my outfit for the occasion, I told her that the baby may take a while and I wanted to be fully ready for this important event in our lives.

But taking a shower? Really?

Although I probably should have acted more like "Johnny-on-the-spot" and ditched the shower and the picking out of clothes, for some reason I had a feeling that this was going to take a while.

And as it turned out, it did take a while. As a matter of fact, Matthew wasn't quite ready to be born just yet. I think he wanted to make a statement about his birth. He felt special, he was the first! "But let's take our time," he said (even though he couldn't yet talk) "as we go about this process, okay?"

So, after a good number of hours (Was it twenty, or did it just seem like that?), the doctor decided that it was time for a Cesarean section.

For those of us who need some schooling on this, a Cesarean section, or C-section as it is sometimes called, is a surgical procedure whereby babies are delivered through an incision in the mother's abdomen oftentimes because a regular vaginal birth would put the mother's and/or the baby's life at risk.

That was part of the reason in Matthew's case, but it also related to the relative sizes of the two parties - mother and son - at the time. As background, Elena was only about five feet tall, with a weight proportionate to her height; however, by the time she was ready to give birth, she had ballooned up by another fifty pounds!

And there was certainly a good reason for that extra fifty pounds, since Matthew himself added his own ten pounds to the equation (Actually it was nine pounds, fifteen ounces but let's not quibble about that extra once, okay?) Matthew plus another forty pounds of related tissue needed to be addressed.

The bottom line was that both baby and mom turned out just fine, although the rest of us were a bit nervous as we awaited the big event.

And, of course, that first C-section had implications for the next Blake baby, Jeffrey, fifteen months down the road.

In that case, I like to think of Jeff as "the planner." He wanted his event to go about on a schedule of his liking. So, he had the doctors plan out his delivery in advance. He seemed to like June 27th as his time, so June 27th it was.

And that delivery went just fine as well. But that second C-section had implications for the mom. It probably wasn't in her interests to go through a third operation of that nature.

So, it was now time to take some precautions. No more babies. No more boys. And no girls, for that matter. Blakes seemed to have a preference for boys at this stage anyway.

And this preference would carry forward when four out of five grandchildren were of the male persuasion, starting almost thirty years later.

Matt and Jamie Blake have three boys, Jake, Noah and Griffin.

And Jeff and Loree also have a boy, Eli, and then, finally, a girl in the person of cute little Camdyn shows up!

Good show, everyone!

Matthew and Jeffrey are the same in many ways. But they are also different in several ways.

Matthew was inclined to go to college as his father did thirty years earlier.

Jeff, on the other hand, wasn't as inclined as Matt. As a matter of fact, he tried a semester at one of the San Mateo CCCD colleges, Canada College. But I don't think he even made it through the end of that semester. He went in another direction.

Matt went to Canada College as well, for the requisite two years, before transferring to Cal Poly San Luis Obispo, and graduating with a business degree. However, after being hired by Wells Fargo, he commented to me one day that he really didn't need that college degree to do his job.

I was disappointed in that observation. I think I told him at the time that he didn't go to college to get a job, rather he did it to get an education. I don't know if he sees that as I do, however. I shouldn't blame him for having that attitude about college and what is derived from the experience. After all, that's all you hear these days: go to college to get a good job.

I think that just about everyone misses the point of a college education. You don't take the history of western civilizations to get a job. You don't take English literature to get a job. You don't take art history to get a job. You take these courses and others in the arts and sciences to get an education.

You take them to be a well-informed person and a good citizen.

If you get a better job because of a degree, that's a nice by-product. Frosting on the cake, so to speak. And that's the "gospel" by Craig Thomas Blake!

While I am proud of my sons' successes in their lives and in their work, and in what they have achieved, I am more proud of them because of what they haven't done.

They never did drugs (at least that I'm aware of). They don't have problems with alcohol abuse. They never got in trouble while in school (although there was one interesting event involving Jeff when he was at Half Moon Bay High School that I'll talk about later). I don't think I, or their mom, was ever contacted by their schools about problems they had with teachers or other students.

Matt has been successful in his Wells Fargo occupation as he climbed the ladder from an entry level position to his job as regional manager in the East Bay.

Jeff has likewise been successful as he maneuvered himself from the trucking industry to plumbing where he also moved up the company ladder.

I am proud of how, with their respective wives, they have "grown" their families. Five great kids.

As well as how they've handled their assets. Early on, Matt was good enough to help Jeff buy a duplex property in which Jeff's family lived in one unit and rented out the other. Ultimately, he sold that property and turned around and bought a very nice single family dwelling in Half Moon Bay which is nearby the children's schools.

Matt, likewise, bought a nice home in Livermore where his boys go to school.

Although Matt and Jeff don't see each other that often, they have supported each other over the years. In addition to their buying a duplex together, Matt got Jeff out of a jam while Jeff was still in high school. That occurred when Jeff was "four-wheeling" on the hillside behind the school, a no-no according to the school principal. Realizing the trouble Jeff might get into, Matt, who had already graduated, told the school people he was the one in the truck that day.

While Jeff decided not to go to a four-year college, he does follow college sports as do I. And he understands my affinity for all things Cal football, getting me a gift of a pen made of wood from the old Cal Memorial stadium stands before they were torn down and replaced with aluminum stands.

I'm hard to please gift-wise, so he scored points with that particular gift. I appreciated it very much.

Although I'll always worry about what the future holds for my boys and their families, I'm confident both sons will weather any storm they may face in the years ahead.

13 - Canines and Felines

I've written quite a bit about a wide variety of folks, Elena, the boys, the grandchildren, relatives and friends alike, and of course, Rhonda. However, and using the perhaps overused, "the story of my life would be incomplete without talking about," I am compelled to address some "folks" I haven't really talked much about so far; and those would be my furry friends, both dogs and cats.

And there have been many of those, maybe a few more cats than dogs, who have been a big part of my life along the way.

I briefly touched on the subject of cats when I mentioned my experience with a cat with a stubby tail. And for the life of me, I still cannot remember that little guy's name. However, there were four felines of mine when I was very young, including "stubby" himself, Prince, Snicker and Pepper. All memorable animals that I missed very much when each of them went off to another world.

With hindsight I wish those animals were totally "inside" rather than "outside" cats at the time since they weren't around all that long. I only now realize that the outside variety live, on average, only two or three years whereas the cats fortunate to live in a house can live upwards of ten years. Obviously, being outside those felines are more subject to the whims of nature as well as accidents.

At this stage of my life, however, I am not finished with felines since we continue to acquire more kitties: ferals or rescues, as well as two cats that I actually paid nine hundred dollars each for.

I wasn't paying much attention to the poor ferals and rescues until I met Rhonda who "educated" me on taking more of an interest in those homeless ones. And I may have forgotten two or three, but to the extent that I can remember, there are the two girls, Lacy and Luna, both of whom are still with us. They are getting up in years now. Also, there is Grayson, the new guy who is only a few years old.

And I shouldn't forget two guys that Rhonda had rescued, Norman and Weasel who, unfortunately, are no longer with us. She had Jinx as well, but he's also gone now.

When Norman, who was a wonderful lap cat, left this Earth, I missed him so much that I named one of the next two after him. Those were the rascals that we drove four hundred miles to get, paying nine hundred each for. While all the other cats in my life were domestic short-hairs, these two, Norman and O.J., were a relatively new breed called "Ragamuffins." When I had read that this breed was known for being great lap cats, I just had to have one, or two as it turned out.

There's a little story there about these two. We drove to southern California initially with the idea of buying the one we named Norman because while he was black, unlike the "original Norman" who was a dark gray, he reminded me a bit of that Norman the First. As Rhonda and I were examining Norman, another black and white Ragamuffin decided he'd like to join in the fun and kept walking around my legs to get my attention. At that point, we decided we needed two lap cats!

So, off we went with $1,800 worth of "lap cats" who didn't, as it turned out, want to be lap cats after all. At least the O.J. one didn't want to remain on a lap. He wanted to be in constant motion. Norman the Second was a bit better as a lap cat although he wouldn't stay on one's lap as long as the first Norman would. That was okay; they both made up for that with their own unique personalities.

We had these two guys when we lived in the Half Moon Bay townhome. And I recall putting O.J. on a leash and taking him for walks outside since he seemed to really want to be an outside cat. On those occasions I got some strange looks from the neighbors.

When we moved to Redding, we took the two Ragamuffins with us for what we hoped would be many, many years. Unfortunately, Norman the Second wasn't as long for this world as we would have liked. One night we found him in the closet behind some clothes crying in pain. We took off for a twenty-four hour veterinary clinic but there was nothing they could do for his condition (of which I do not recall the name) and we had no choice but to have him "put to sleep."

I was obviously very sad and it was the first time in memory as an adult that I cried over the loss of a pet.

We still have O.J. and hope that despite his age at this point we will have him for a few more years. We are concerned, however, about his weight. Even for a Ragamuffin, his twenty-four pounds is a bit on the heavy side. So, our vet helped us by putting him on a diet. And O.J. is losing those pounds slowly, but surely.

Having addressed most of the felines in my life, I turn now to the canine variety, of whom I've had only a very few. Actually, I had only one dog when I was younger. We were a cat family, not a dog family. I'm not sure why that was the case, maybe because I never asked to have a dog.

We wouldn't have had that one dog, however, if my brother Reid hadn't brought him home one day. Apparently the dog was hanging out near Reid's workplace, a plumbing business in San Rafael, and Reid decided the poor animal needed a home.

I think my parents were a little taken aback at the sight of the dog we decided to name "Bruno." He was a small black Cocker mix. Very furry and very friendly. Again, he was another outside animal although we kept him safely in the back of the garage at night.

We did not have Bruno for a very long time, maybe two years at best when one sad morning I went out to give him his breakfast, and found that poor Bruno had died.

I can't remember if I cried, but I probably did.

No more dogs in my life after that, at least my life as a youngster. That was until I was married and had two grown boys. Jeff, the younger of the two decided he wanted a Rottweiler who he named Daisy.

I'm embarrassed to say that I don't remember a lot about Daisy, largely because she was really Jeff's dog. At this point I can't even remember when Daisy passed on. It may have been when Jeff had his own place in Half Moon Bay, but I'm not sure of that. I do know that poor Daisy had an untreatable cancer causing Jeff to have her put down. I'm sure that was a difficult time for Jeff.

So the next stage of "dogdom" is here in Redding. As I already mentioned, we have several cats inside. And we care and feed for several more outside. I didn't mention it, but presently we have only two ferals, named "Shadow" and "Reggie." We recently lost another guy named "Eddie." The problem with ferals is that they tend to come and go over time, subject to the same hazards as the outside cats that I had as a child.

The canine idea was somewhat similar to my desire to have a special cat breed, the Ragamuffin. I believe it was after I watched the movie about an Akita, *Hachi, a Dog's Tale*, that I decided I needed to have a dog with such fierce loyalty as the one Richard Gere had.

The movie had quite a sad ending when Richard Gere died (the character, not the actor of course). Hachi had been going to his owner's train station at the end of every work day to greet him until the day the latter passed on. But that didn't preclude Hachi from continuing to go to that station every day, even in the snow.

I just had to have one of these animals.

So, that's when our "Zeus" came on board. I had searched and searched for an Akita until the point where I realized I wasn't going to find one locally. So I did an on-line search all over the country, eventually finding a breeder – I think it was in Mississippi - that had several Akita puppies ready for adoption. These Akitas were what is called the American variety. They're slightly different in coloration than the Japanese kind which are called Akita Innu. So, sight unseen, only pictures, I selected one named Zeus and had him shipped to California where I picked him up in his crate at the San Francisco airport.

He was such a handful even then that I would have sent him back except Rhonda came to his rescue as she exclaimed, "Don't I have a say in the matter?"

End of story. We kept him. And we decided that "Zeus" was a perfect name for him. Zeus is the "God of Gods." So we kept the name.

We decided that since Zeus loved to run around so much, we needed a larger area than was already available for such activity and so we had a nice wrought iron fence constructed around the backyard with a resulting extra quarter acre of running area for him.

And as I write this, Zeus is barking his head off, which he does quite a lot of these days. I'm not quite sure what got him going this time. Probably the arrival of one of the "outside" cats that we feed daily.

I would be less than candid, however, if I didn't address one of Zeus's shortcomings. He is extremely protective of his food stuffs, particularly his Nubs bones. I've had more than one negative experience with him in that regard.

And the other night, Rhonda was on the receiving end of his overreaction, this time due to her attempting to examine what item he had on the carpet. Whamo! He hauled off and bit her twice on her left forearm. It drew blood which we attempted to address with appropriate peroxide and then some gauze and bandages.

Over our continued concern, however, we decided to go to the local emergency for a more scrutinous procedure.

What we got was probably not worth the trip, as the medical folks merely rebandaged the wounds, charging $465 for their efforts.

And we were, unfortunately, put on notice that Zeus needed to be licensed and quarantined for two weeks.

Nonetheless, I still love him, but I have to wonder whether Rhonda still feels the same way as that day, upon his arrival, when she said, "Don't I have a say in the matter?"

Personally, I hope he'll be around for a few more years. Or at least as long as I am.

Fifth Piece: Looking to the Future

1 - Ruminations on the Future

Where is life headed for me now?

I like to plan. However, what I plan on and what happens are not necessarily the same thing, are they?

My dad certainly didn't plan on dying in 1976 at the relatively young age of 65, but he did. He died of leukemia that year. The doctors failed to uncover that acute disease until rather late in its development. I wish they caught on to that sooner and were able to do something for him.

My brother lived a little longer than my dad, but he certainly didn't plan on dying in 2016 at age 74, but he did. From a heart attack, not knowing he had a heart condition to begin with. I wish he had regular physicals but he didn't.

Fortunately, my mom managed to make it to age 82. But she never planned on dying of pancreatic cancer at the time. In my father's case, I had done my research on his leukemia. I hadn't done the proper research on my mom's form of cancer and I should have. When she told me that it was very serious, I thought she was overreacting at the time. But she wasn't, was she? Rather, I was underreacting.

I do recall the day she passed away. I was working at the San Mateo County Community College District at the time when Elena and I were living in our home in Ocean Colony. Elena had been good enough to go to my mom's home at the time since mom wasn't doing all that well, and for that I will always be very grateful. I continued to go to work, not really thinking that she would shortly pass on. Mom's husband, Frank, was at a point in his life where some form of dementia was clearly setting in on him. I don't know what I would have done had it not been for Elena's concern for mom and her care.

The day before my mom passed away, Elena called me very early in the morning to tell me she didn't think my mother was going to last much longer. I was stunned by her call. I told Elena I would get there ASAP.

Now, this is one of those times when I can't believe what I next did. I actually got up, got showered and dressed, and proceeded to go to my District office, and spend about two hours addressing some "loose ends."

Stupid, stupid, stupid!

When your mom is near death, you don't hesitate. You don't take a shower. And you most certainly don't go to your work place, "loose ends" or not. Anyone reading this please listen very carefully, particularly my sons if you are reading this. If your mother is near death do only what you really need to do that day. Most of all don't go to work! Work doesn't need you, but your mother does.

Don't be as thoughtless as I was. If you are, you won't like the outcome, I can tell you.

The reason I say this is because when I finally arrived at her home in San Pablo, a thirty mile drive from San Mateo, my mother barely recognized me. By then she was near death.

I was beside myself at the time, almost instantly regretting the two or three hours I had taken to get ready, to go to work, and then to drive to her home.

My mom was barely holding on; I think every last ounce of her being was waiting for the only son she was in contact with to arrive so she could say goodbye to that son.

She passed away sometime during the night or the next morning. And it was particularly sad because I don't think her husband, Frank, who was lying next to her when she died, even realized she was gone. I don't know which was sadder, her death or her husband not being emotionally with her in her final moments.

So, I'll return to the concept of planning.

One can make plans; however, one must also be aware of how what I would call "externalities" can frustrate those plans. Does that mean I'm a pessimist? No, I would call myself a "realist," who thinks in terms of what prior experiences of other family members impacted their lives and their plans.

My dad planned on retiring to a little cabin on a lake somewhere. He liked lakes. Which made sense since he came from the state of Minnesota, the "land of 10,000 lakes." As absurd as it may sound, my dad told me that that figure was actually on the low side.

I'm not quite sure of the plans my brother Reid had, if any. Probably at least to continue his passions of collecting his rifles (he had quite a few in a large safe in his home), hunting, shooting, or just hanging out with his buddies. He had a cowboy outfit and was part of a group called, "The Richmond Rough Riders," each member of which had a "handle" or reference to their cowboy-like pursuits. Reid's was "Whiskey Rivers." I don't know where that came from but it sounds pretty cool to me. From time to time, I pull out a card he gave me, showing him in his cowboy regalia holding a rifle and wearing a side arm as well. He truly looked the part of the character, "Whiskey Rivers."

Recently, I ran across something called a life expectancy calculator which was developed by John Hancock Insurance Company. According to that calculator, I could expect to live to the ripe old age of 101, but only with some fairly precarious assumptions. Like maintaining normal blood pressure. And exercising every day which I do not.

That's interesting because ten years ago, a doctor told me I probably had a good twenty more years in me. Using that as a predictor would mean I'd live to about eighty-four years. Now that I'm age 74, that seems like a short period.

The Hancock calculator predicts that I could live to the age of 95 if I have normal blood pressure, but don't exercise daily. And it's also 95 if I have high blood pressure, but mitigate it with daily exercise.

It drops to 89 if my blood pressure is high and I don't exercise at all. That's still a good fifteen years away from my current point in time.

Can I rely on these projections? Probably not. For all kinds of reasons. Those zingers that come out of nowhere. Like accidents. Although the Hancock calculator does consider whether you've had any automobile accidents in the last five years in its projections. That could be a kind of proxy for how you lead your life in general.

It's unclear to me how Hancock factors in things like heart attacks and strokes, two of the causes of death that can come out of nowhere as was the case for my brother Reid.

How does the calculator factor in leukemia disease, which was the ultimate cause of my dad's death?

And as I said, accidents come out of nowhere. In my case, a fall from a ladder I had when I lived in Half Moon Bay could have killed me. Fortunately for me, it didn't.

I had Covid-19 in February of this year and it was severe. I was lucky it didn't kill me. Did Hancock factor Covid into its calculations? It likely couldn't since Covid-19 came about years after the calculator was first developed.

As far as those things that Hancock does consider, every time I drive down and back from the Bay Area, a five hundred mile round trip, I realize I could have an accident that would kill me. Particularly when I change lanes, going to the right. That's always a challenge for me, not sure why, however.

And there's more to consider coming up.

2 - The Life Expectancy "Game"

Having gone through all of the aforementioned, now let's play a game which goes like this. You decide which of those John Hancock projections seems to make the most sense. Living one year past the century mark doesn't seem all that realistic. Largely due to all the "zingers" that I've already discussed.

Even living to the grand old age of 95 doesn't seem that realistic. For more than one reason. Also, have you seen anyone lately who is either 95 or 101 years of age? They don't look all that hot, do they?

So, is 89 the magic number? What would you do with your remaining fifteen years if you knew that's when you'd take off for that next level? I try not to give that kind of thing much thought, and I don't know if I really like the idea of knowing when I'll die.

Once, my friend Guati and I debated what some may consider a philosophical issue. He argued that he'd like to know when he would die. When I asked him why he wished to know this, his response was he would have sex with as many ladies as possible up to that very last moment.

Now that may apply to someone who is in their twenties as was Guati at the time we had this discussion. And let's assume that the "death date" was not all that far away. However, when one is talking in terms of the eighties, nineties and the really outlandish age of 101, does one really believe they will be engaged in such activities?

Even if you could, you'd still need a ready and willing partner. There may not be a lot of those at that age. That is, unless you're operating on the really grandiose assumption that your partner will be in their twenties, thirties or forties.

Dream on, my friend.

Let's next pretend that there are all sorts of other non-lovemaking activities that you wish to engage in up until the magic number. You could wrap your plans around that notion and proceed.

If I'm still pursuing stuff that I do at present, that could involve activities such as collecting coins, gazing at the stars, pounding the ivories, and writing novels (and maybe even one more memoir!).

I could even try to get one published through a mainstream publisher!

Probably no drag racing or scuba diving. Or maybe just a little of those. Sailing is still a possibility, but you'd definitely need a first mate. You don't want to end up like Robert Redford did in his movie, "All is Lost," do you? Did you see that one? If you haven't, you should.

So there are some things that you could continue to pursue, maybe even adding some other stuff that's been on your bucket list but you just haven't got there yet.

What could those be?

I can tell you for sure what is not on that list. No skydiving! You'll never get me to do what both of my sons have done: jump tandem out of a plane not really sure you're not going "splat" (in the words of my friend, Ted) when you reach terra ferma.

I might be willing to go into space with Jeff Bezos or Richard Branson, but only if I had the requisite million dollars or so.

No solo climbing. No base jumping. No wing suiting. No hang gliding.

Mountain climbing? It's a possibility but I probably wouldn't have the necessary stamina at even 89 years of age.

Anyway, maybe there are no bucket list items for me to consider.

In any case, there is another consideration relating to any of these activities: your "golden age" budget. As is the case with rocketing into space, some of these are more costly than others. For example, the last time I looked, coin collecting started to get prohibitively expensive. How did this come about? Well, it's probably because I purchased all the least expensive coins early on in the process. So, the ones I haven't yet bought are in the range from $2,000 each on up.

Also, writing novels that are self-published can get rather pricey. Recently, I expended about thirty-eight hundred dollars doing that with two novels in quick succession. It can be accomplished at lower cost if you do a more down-scale version of it. But you're going to spend at least $800 per novel. Unless, of course, you find a publishing company that is willing to pay you, rather than visa-versa.

Which, in my case, is not very likely.

So, where am I at the present time with the writing process? Rather than work on a novel, *Dark Arrivals*, that was a sequel to the previous one, *Dark Futures*, I already mentioned that I recently lost interest and that's when I decided to go the memoir route. Once I complete this writing effort, I'm not sure if I'll return to *Dark Arrivals,* or try my hand at something entirely different in the field of writing.

We'll see.

So far I've limited my "ruminations on the future" to those things which I have control over.

What about the stuff over which I have little if any control? There are a lot of those. What are they? Perhaps I should consider what the "futurists" – the folks who predict the future for a living - have to say on the matter.

Some predict much more leisure time. That won't apply to me since I have all the leisure time I need as a retiree from the world of work.

Others predict increased time spent on-line by the work force. Again, doesn't apply here.

Almost all futurists, and many non-futurists, predict negative impacts on society due to climate change. Will Foster City in the Bay Area be inundated with water? More importantly, here in Redding, what will the future climate be like? I've already considered climate change and have noted that much of the northwest is seeing its summer temperatures soaring. Such as places like Seattle and Portland witnessing temperatures of over 110 degrees.

In Redding, we're used to that sort of thing. However, what's different this time around is the heat is coming on earlier than usual. In June of 2021, we're seeing temperatures well over 100 degrees. It's hard to be a climate change denier in the present environment.

Let's turn away from climate change and consider what Ray Kurzweil, a noted futurist, has to say on the matter of future change. After all, I've read that he's been correct 86 percent of the time in his past predictions.

Kurzweil predicts that by the year 2045, the "singularity" will be upon us. What is that? Well, the singularity is the point in time when technology such as artificial intelligence is smarter than us humans.

Well, that's twenty-four years in the future which would make me ninety-eight years old if I were still alive, that is. That's in the high range of my own life expectancy, so maybe I shouldn't fret over that. Right?

Wrong. Because Kurzweil also predicts that by the year 2029, just eight years from now, technology will be just as smart as us humans. I will or would be eighty-two years of age which is actually less than my worst case John Hancock life expectancy of eighty-nine.

Does that mean I should worry about technology's advancement? Not necessarily, since the most obvious impacts will be to non-retirees. The work force in many fields will be replaced by machines.

Ah, but there are some related predictions that could positively impact those of us who are getting up in years. By the early 2030s, Kurzweil says we will be able to copy the human consciousness onto an electronic medium. So what, you ask? Well, it has implications for human life. With this type of advancement, humans will no longer have to rely on their fragile biology. We could live forever!

Let's see. Hmm. The early twenty-thirties would put me at eighty-four to eighty-six years of age. That's below the ages predicted by Hancock's life expectancy for me.

Related to Kurzweil's forecast is one made by Elon Musk. He claims that many of the diseases that plague humanity will be eliminated during the current early twenties given the medical breakthroughs that are coming about. Maybe that could address some of those "zingers" I was talking about a little earlier?

It makes one think. If these medical breakthroughs impacting lives as much as some predict, then will John Hancock have to significantly revise its life expectancy tables?

Some food for thought as I continue to look for the answer to the original question. Now what was the question? I don't seem to remember.

Just kidding.

3 - And the Afterlife

Having speculated a bit on what the future might hold for me, I still need to address what I will call some "loose ends" in that future world, things I continue to think about, but so far haven't done much about. And I really need to.

Starting with what should my loved ones (probably my partner Rhonda, unless she predeceases me) do with me when I am no longer of this Earth?

That's another way of saying "when I die," which I don't like to use.

Anyway, I guess there's burial. If so, it would be more than appropriate to have me as near as possible to my parent's grave sites. That would be at St. Joseph's Cemetery in San Pablo, California. However, that may be a little costly since it's about 225 miles from Redding.

I plan to leave enough money behind to cover such things.

And then there's cremation. That's less expensive but as one baptized in the Roman Catholic (RC) religion (even though

I don't seem to practice it much anymore), I tend to steer away from that approach (Or do they allow that now?).

Do I want a service to take place in a church? That would be nice, but I don't think anyone would come. And that's not meant as a joke. Either I'm too far away at my current Redding address from those who could be invited, or the folks I knew in the past are dead and gone now. That is the case, of course, since death is a frequent visitor with folks about my age.

I recall when my mom died, I found her phone directory and diligently went about the process of identifying all those people I thought she might want at her service and her burial at St. Joseph's Cemetery. So, I called them all. And many of them came.

Regarding my father's situation, there's a funny story there (Or maybe a sad story?). I recall the day vividly. It was a quite beautiful day, very sunny and warm. My mom and I drove to the Catholic church in Santa Venetia. We left early so we could get a good parking spot.

As we approached the parking lot, we saw that there already were a lot of cars there; we would need to park in an adjoining lot.

While it was inconvenient, my mom was heartened at all the people who apparently came to my dad's funeral service. She had a little smile on her face.

As we walked to the church, we noticed something odd though. The church goers were exiting the church! My mom was taken aback, as was I.

That is, until we realized that "all the people" who came to my dad's funeral were actually attending a Mass that always takes place at that particular hour.

That was a bit of a letdown.

Fortunately, many people did attend his service after all, just not as many, however, as had been at Mass. And that's the way it should have been since my father had made friends with many of the customers who shopped in his market.

Another important issue that surrounds one's demise is "who gets what?" Those being all the things of value that are left behind.

There is a way to address all of these considerations; it's called a "will" or, better yet, a "living trust."

That item should be at the top of my bucket list for the hereafter, so to speak. Hopefully, that also will be taken care of ASAP.

One more thing. Although not saying it at the outset, and rethinking what I did say, I believe the most "valuable" possession I have to pass on is this memoir itself. I don't know how to assign a dollar value to it, but it definitely has value.

And in my mind it certainly is the most meaningful possession that I can offer.

4 - Reflections on the Past

I mentioned in my prologue that I hoped to find answers to life's important questions through the process of writing itself. Although I hope any readers of this memoir may gain something from it, I too would like to benefit from it.

I've already begun to examine what needs to be addressed upon my demise. And I will continue to ponder that.

There is an unintended consequence of this process, however, and it makes me realize even more than I did before that my memory is beginning to fail me in more than one way.

I don't think it's as dire as Alzheimer's or other forms of dementia, but it continues to be a concern of mine. It's certainly a concern of Rhonda's. Particularly on those days that I ask her about something that she has already told me about. I'm sure that's difficult for her. She probably fears that I am heading in the direction of a serious form of dementia.

As a result, I've done some googling on the nature of memory itself. I've learned that there are all kinds of memories with different ways to classify those memories.

One way suggests that there are three basic kinds of memories: working memory, short-term memory and long-term memory. Working memory has been described as being able to work with information without losing track of it. One person described it as being like a temporary "sticky note" attached to the brain. As such it holds information in place so that the brain can work with it briefly, connecting it with other information.

Working memory isn't just for short-term use; it also helps the brain to organize new information for long-term use.

Sometimes working memory and short-term memory are used interchangeably, however, some hold that they are different from each other. As such, short-term memory has been described as being a kind of cognitive system that is used for holding sensory events, movements and cognitive information such as digits, words, names and other items for a brief period of time. Some would say this is the same as working memory. Others claim it is somewhat different.

Finally, long term memory refers to the storage of information for an extended period of time.

Now that I have defined the three terms, let me try to suggest the implications of different forms of memory with respect to information included in this memoir.

For the past several years, I've felt that both my working memory and my short-term memory were beginning to fail me as I go about my activities. An example being that I can't recall where I placed a magazine or newspaper that I had just a few seconds or a few minutes earlier.

And as I've already noted, there are times when I have to ask my partner about something that she has apparently already told me about earlier. This can be quite frustrating for both of us. And also it's not always clear whether I heard what she told me in the first place.

I will readily admit that many times I'm just not paying enough attention to what is being said by the speaker.

So, the apparent "memory problem" becomes confused with a hearing problem. Rhonda continually tells me I should get my hearing checked. My counter to that is that I already know I have a hearing impairment. And it is the type of impairment that cannot be addressed by a hearing aid. I don't know if there's a name for this particular condition, but I tend to confuse consonants, such as mistaking the word "cat" for the word "hat." Apparently, it relates to an inability to hear at higher frequencies. And I'm told by some audiologists that a hearing aid will merely magnify the problem, not correct it.

I've come to accept these related memory problems and hearing problems. And I've tried various "tricks" to mitigate them. Nonetheless, I continue to have these problems.

Having considered working and/or short-term memories, let me turn to the long-term aspect of memory. An example of a kind of long-term memory problem in my case became apparent when I was trying to recall certain events that I'm writing about in my memoir. I first became aware of this when

I went back to try and reconstruct the events that led to my decision to find an orthodontist and then to use his services.

The steps involved were as follows: First, learning of my order-of-call for induction to military service; second, encountering another student who informed me of a potential deferment; third, returning to the SF Bay Area; and lastly, identifying an orthodontist there who agreed to take me on.

On the internet I pulled up information relating to the time of the draft lottery itself. Based on that date, there was something not right about the order in which I thought those four steps occurred.

And that something appears to be where I encountered the dental student who informed me about a possible deferment. It would have been impossible for a student at UCLA to advise me on that aspect since the draft lottery occurred after the time I was at UCLA.

I know, however, that I'm right about the type of student he was. He definitely was a dentistry or pre-dentistry student, otherwise why would he be advising me on something related to orthodontics?

And something else, the UC Berkeley campus doesn't have a dental program; that would be UCSF, which does.

So, where and when did I encounter this particular student?

Overall, I'm convinced that those steps did indeed happen; however, their relationship to each other and when exactly they took place is my conundrum. Not enough for me to throw out the whole discussion, but enough to make me aware that something wasn't quite right.

However, the reader should know I'm leaving that part of the memoir as is, since I believe it involves one or more "lessons" about life that are important. And they have nothing to do with whether I got the timing of those events right.

The reason I bring this up is to point out that at my age the aspects of some long-term events relative to the time they occurred are not necessarily accurate. And this does bother me as it no doubt should.

And that means that my reflections on bits and pieces of my life are based on what I think happened, not necessarily on what actually took place.

Now I understand that this is a relatively common situation. There have even been experiments conducted in which multiple individuals witness an event and then later they are asked to reconstruct that event. Inevitably, not all of the parties agree with each other.

Those kinds of experiments involve short-term memory; however, there are long-term implications associated with such experiments. If you don't have a correct understanding of what happened in the short-term, then that can carry over into the future when you reflect upon that event.

And that may have, indeed, happened with respect to my current recall of the UCLA to UC Berkeley transition that took place over fifty years ago.

5 - Worry Wart

Beginning in the late 1920s, a character called "Worry Wart" appeared in Dell comics. Of course, I wasn't around then but I've read that this little guy wasn't a worrier at all; he was a nuisance, an annoyance, causing others to worry.

While he is no longer in the comics, we still have things like "Worry Wart" hanging over us a lot of the time. And granted, some tend to worry more than others. In its most extreme version, worrying has been referred to as "generalized anxiety disorder" (GAD). It has a cousin called "obsessive compulsive disorder" (OCD).

Whether one is characterized as having GAD or OCD, these are extreme conditions in which either worry gets out of hand or becomes a compulsion, a kind of obsession over something that a "normal" person would not feel.

We all experience degrees of worry and sometimes a bit of obsession with something in our environment. This is normal behavior; however, when we lose control in dealing with worry, we begin to move toward that state of GAD. And, as such, some would uncharitably characterize us as "worry warts." Again, it's only a problem if we allow it to get out of hand in the manner in which we address whatever our worry is about.

I sometimes refer to myself as a worry wart. I sometimes refer to others as worry warts. However, I don't think of myself as having GAD or OCD. I don't necessarily think that the folks I deem to be worry warts have either of these two disorders either.

But there are other times when I begin to think that my worrying is getting out of hand. It's taking control of my life and unless I take some necessary action, something bad is going to happen. If I have grounds for feeling this way, my level of concern may be appropriate. The issue then becomes what am I going to do about it?

This is probably the appropriate stage of this part of the memoir to address the concept of "worry." Especially since the last episode reflected on my past and the next will focus on the lessons learned from my past.

If I have your attention at this point, that's a good thing since I believe you may learn something from my experiences with "worry."

What do I worry about? Lots of things. Oftentimes, I have worried about occupational situations as the one wherein my boss asked me, "You're not nervous are you?" Eventually I learned what that meant and from that point on I did become more concerned or uneasy about my work world when things just weren't going the way I had hoped.

But again, it's what you do about it that's important. You don't "stew in your juices," rather you define the cause of your worry and then move full steam ahead to address whatever brought that about. In the case of the work world, you have at least two options: one, resolve what is bringing on the worry, or two, start looking for employment elsewhere.

I have another example which may prove illustrative of how to go about handling worry outside of the work world. Sometime earlier in my narrative I discussed my pastime of sailing. Actually, it wasn't merely a pastime, it was more of a passion. So much so that ultimately I decided to buy my own sailboat. Of which there were some pluses and some minuses.

The pluses are fairly obvious if you enjoy sailing on a nearby lake. Also obvious are the minuses such as the upkeep and costs associated with that upkeep.

However, there was a negative about it that I only began to appreciate after I bought my MacGregor sailboat and had it delivered to Whiskeytown Lake. And earlier I think I likened it to "leaving your baby in a stroller and walking away."

The MacGregor was my "baby." And I left it docked or anchored all by its lonesome self out on the Lake. It seemed like there wasn't a moment when I didn't worry about it. I'm reluctant to call it an obsession because of the implications of thinking in those terms. I don't think of myself as an obsessive-compulsive type of person. However, it was so close to that level of concern that I knew I had to take some kind of action. One obvious way to alleviate that concern would have been to live on it as some folks do with their sailboats. However, that was not practical, either in terms of my own comforts or the Whiskeytown Lake authorities allowing that in the first place.

Eliminating that option, what others did I have? Paying someone to watch over it for me? Probably just as impractical as the prior idea.

I eventually came to the only resolution that made sense; if I couldn't rise above my seeming obsession about leaving it all by itself, I needed to get rid of the boat. So, I placed an advertisement and shortly found a buyer who paid me a fair price. My rationalization was that I got a year's worth of use out of the boat, probably close to covering the costs of renting one over the same period. And if I missed sailing, after selling it, I could always rent one.

To another more disinterested party, this may sound strange, but as soon as that boat and its trailer left the Lake it was like having a gigantic weight lifted from my chest. Not to mention the tidy sum I received and banked.

There are other sources of worry. For example, I worry about being infected by the so-called Covid Delta Variant that is going around. That's another reasonable kind of worry given that I was knocked out by the original Covid for over two months and I wasn't looking forward to a repeat of that experience (assuming I could be reinfected).

So, even though I've been vaccinated, I still wear a mask wherever I go since being vaccinated doesn't necessarily preclude being infected.

There's another reason to wear a mask at this time (although it requires a different type of mask for protection): There have been a considerable number of fires nearby this summer. Two of them, the McFarland fire and the Monument fire, although several miles from our home, have burned an amount of acreage approaching one million total.

And, as I speak, yet another fire has broken out closer to home. It's called the Fawn fire (in the Lake Shasta area) and it was apparently set by a woman from Palo Alto, who the week before had been arrested in Oregon for a different type of crime.

Of course, there is always the worry associated with just how close to us those fires will come. We've been in that predicament almost every year, but fortunately we managed to escape those fires. And concomitant with those fires is the smoke that lingers around our house as well as much of the Redding area. Wearing a mask now takes on another underlying reason, particularly for those who have experienced pulmonary problems in the past.

Other sources of worry for me. Last night I found a foxtail in my Akita Zeus and was not getting his cooperation in removing it. And it was late, and I was tired, so I went to bed resolving to deal with it in the morning. Problem was, I couldn't easily get to sleep since I was worried that the foxtail would get even more embedded in his skin.

My concern was greatly alleviated when I arose to learn that Rhonda was able to remove it when she arose much earlier than I.

Maybe I should adopt that approach more often. That would solve a multitude of problems, wouldn't it? Let someone else deal with the problem. I'm half kidding, yet oftentimes many of us do embrace such a tactic.

Another example. I was called to jury duty several months ago when I had the Covid-19. I called and got a postponement of that service which worked out well. Unfortunately, I got another notice in the mail a few weeks ago. And I happened to have a doctor's appointment the same day. My doctor is a specialist and if you cancel an appointment it's not easy to get another one shortly after the canceled appointment.

So, I called and left a message saying I had a conflict with a medical appointment. However, the automated response told me I already had a postponement and I couldn't have another. So, I did attempt to reschedule that appointment and was successful. However, the night before my jury duty was scheduled I was very tired and didn't really feel like getting up at six a.m. to go to court the next day.

What did I do? I ended up sleeping in the next morning, prepared to deal with whatever consequences came my way as a result.

That's where the inevitable worry wart in me kicked in, particularly when I read that part of my jury service card reading, "failure to appear could result in a fine and/or incarceration."

However, shortly thereafter I switched from "worry mode" to "indignant mode." I said to myself, I'm not some common criminal. I'm an upstanding citizen of the community. How dare they threaten me with fines and incarceration! I'll sue them if they take action!

Of course, I shortly came to my senses and reasoned that being indignant probably wasn't going to wash with the authorities.

There was a happy ending to this escapade. My partner had filed a request for exemption from service altogether since I was age 74 with a history of lung problems which would cause my appearance at the court to be highly risky. And within twenty four hours, I received a call from the "jury exemptor" (Is that a word?) saying that my request was approved and I need never to report for jury service thereafter.

Another good example of letting someone else handle whatever was worrying me. In this case it was the same person as the last incident. If such behavior continues that other person is probably going to get just a little annoyed with me.

But still, I like that approach. I think I'll use that tactic more frequently!

But probably with someone else inheriting my concern.

6 - Lessons to be Learned

Assuming that my memories related to the timing of events or of what transpired during those events are accurate, there are lessons to be learned from those memories.

Let's start with the "In the Beginning" part of my story. And let's take the simple example of my being told when I was very young that our family changed our names from "Block" to "Blake" because "mean people called us 'blockheads.'"

I went a good fifty plus years never questioning that. It wasn't until I started a family genealogy investigation more recently that I discovered my father must have been kidding me, or perhaps that he had been seriously misinformed about the Blake lineage.

Why did I take those fifty plus years to look into that? After all, it was a fairly serious allegation about mean people and the effect they can have on our lives. It's not terribly important that these "mean people" called us blockheads; what's important was to get the story right from the beginning.

Another good example relates to the episode about, "A New World." Why did I have to "fall into the world of teaching" to figure out that there were more enjoyable occupations than administrating? I had some teaching experience on a part-time basis and enjoyed it. Why didn't that tell me something? Why hadn't I considered other lines of work along the way rather than stumbling from one administrator job to the next?

Of course, at this point that's water under the bridge. However, maybe those younger readers who take a peek at my experience will spend more time thinking about what they do and why they do it. Maybe they should ask themselves from time to time if there is something else of more value to them than the work they are currently engaged in.

Also relating to the world of work were my experiences at the San Mateo CCCD. I believe I had already made the observation in the relevant passage, but I will underscore that observation with the lesson that one needs to be very careful in terms of personal relationships with subordinates.

I should have been more thoughtful of the consequences at the time or at least understood the implications associated with my behavior.

And that lesson can be applied to other work relationships beyond subordinates. There's always an opportunity for jealousy interfering with your best intentions if you don't have your guard up.

Probably my dad losing his job had one of the biggest impacts on me. Whether consciously or not, I have always been guarded about the potential loss of one of my jobs.

Maybe that is why I was always, "looking for the next big advancement," whereas in reality I was fearful of an outcome such as my father experienced.

It prepared me for the inevitable when organizations founder and it impacts one's job security. It's a lesson that applied to my history with employers like A.T. Kearney and Aerojet Composites. While I wasn't quite prepared for the "inevitable" outcome with the former organization, the lesson was not lost on me regarding the latter. And it strengthened my resolve in those cases to soldier on despite the situation.

Outside of work, there are other examples of my experiences that have caused me to view things with a more questioning mind. My parents' purchase of the home on the creek has stuck with me over time and causes me to be more aware of hazards of homes that I've considered buying. I certainly learned a valuable lesson from their experience.

Another lesson involves my brother passing away from a condition he may have had and didn't even realize it. That should give me pause every time I note a physical condition of my own that doesn't seem quite right. Get it checked out.

Here's something else to ponder. This one involves assuming things. Don't go around making assumptions without a good basis for making those assumptions in the first place. Case in point: my assumption that I would not be accepted into the UC Berkeley Graduate School of Business if I applied. I should have given that more thought than I did at the time. And if I still didn't have a good handle on my potential acceptance, I should have simply applied to the School and taken my chances.

Nothing ventured, nothing gained, as the expression goes.

Which actually makes me think about another of my assumptions. Why am I self-publishing novels in the first place? Why haven't I tried to utilize a mainstream publisher? Why haven't I tried to get an agent who could find a publisher for me? Is it too outlandish to believe that my works are not up to snuff to pursue that avenue?

I've been assuming that my books haven't been selling because I have seen no increase in the number of reviews that my novels have garnered. However, just today I received an accounting of my royalties for the past year. The total dollar amount reflects sales for Kindle, soft cover and hard cover versions of all three novels and they are considerably higher than they had been in the past.

I failed to realize that book reviews are not always an accurate gauge of sales; they merely reflect those readers who took the time to write a review. I'd like more reviews, but in their absence, I'll certainly accept more sales.

And I'll continue to think about finding an agent that could assist me in that regard.

The episode about, "Reaching Out to Reid," certainly makes me rethink the time when he fell out of favor with our parents and, unfortunately, me as well. Why did I allow that to happen?

Why did I have to take sides? Why didn't I just keep seeing my brother after that happened?

Would that have been the end of the world? I don't think so.

And my last observation involves a lesson relating to my friendship with Ted. I saw all the signs of a person in trouble. Why didn't I do something about that? I literally abandoned him and I shouldn't have. It's too late to help Ted, unfortunately, but that lesson could still be applied to others.

Epilogue:
Finding One's Niche

Some final thoughts.

One of the advantages of "old age" is the ability to see the forest for the trees. In the prior episode I did a bit of this. In this one I'd like to underscore what I've already observed: that is, how we can reflect on our lives and examine those aspects which should have tipped us off, so to speak, as to where we could have gone at a given time but, unfortunately, did not.

This leads me to the topic of abilities. Now, one measure of our abilities, at least while we're in school, is the grades we achieve. In the work world, the "grades" are the evaluations we receive from others, both superiors as well as other "graders" (such as students whose opinions we seek as teachers).

Starting with our schooling, we should be able to determine what we're good at and what we're not good at. I have to be honest, while I was in high school my grades overall were fairly unexceptional. True, I was a little better at some subjects than others. As I reflect, I note that my highest grades were in

"Spanish" and, ironically, "Religion." I say ironically, because I seem to have fallen away from my faith.

I also noted that my grades trended upward as the years went by. I guess I was learning how to psych out the system, so to speak.

But I also realized I didn't perform well in those subjects requiring memory skills, that is the ability to recall dates, names, places and other factual considerations. Thus, I needed to rely more on rote learning in subjects like "History" or "Biology."

As an example I had a fairly young, albeit capable history instructor over those four years who also taught sociology; unfortunately, he put too much emphasis on what are called "objective" questions such as true/false, multiple choice, or one word answers. An example being: "What year did the Battle of Hastings take place," rather than asking a subjective and more probing essay question such as: "Why was the Battle of Hastings important to the participants?"

As an instructor myself, I understand why he asked that type of question since answers were penciled onto a Scantron form, making the grading of five or six classes that much easier for him. (My apologies to an instructor named "Jim"' who we referred to by his last name.)

So much for this digression; the point I'm trying to make is that those grades should have told me what direction I should go in, or what I should have emphasized later in life.

However, in my case that didn't work very well since my grades were pretty much clustered together, no one subject area rose well above the others; I wasn't a star in "Mathematics" or in "English Literature."

So, I entered post-secondary education lacking a clear guideline on what I should emphasize, other than knowing I would always be challenged in subjects requiring recall.

That may be commonplace for many students and likely the reason why the first two years of college aren't the time to specialize in anything in particular. However, as we "sample" various subject fields, we begin to get a better gauge on what we should emphasize in the last two years, and/or what "major" we should go for.

But once again, nothing rose to the top for me. So, I had to engage in a trial and error approach, first trying out "Engineering" because it sounded interesting. (With hindsight, I have to say that majors should not necessarily be selected merely because they sound "interesting.")

Besides, that major was challenged by a case of mononucleosis I had developed, coupled with a serious depression, leaving me out on the street.

Once I was back at Cal, however, I went "trial and error" again, going through three different majors until I landed in "Business," a field I always thought was a haven for football players and other student athletes, not for serious-minded students. After all, when I was finally able to have access to the scores associated with various skill tests I took in high school (and formerly confidential), I learned that I was in the 91st percentile in mental ability and had an IQ of 126. Not MENSA level, but certainly a clear cut above the norm.

That tells me that I just wasn't really applying myself, was I?

In any case, once I arrived at the Business School, I learned that I could actually excel at something, garnering almost straight "A"s.

So, I finally found my niche. And that pointed me in a clear direction; I should continue in the field of business by seeking the MBA degree. And I did just that, and completed the program with grades approaching a 4.0 GPA.

At that point, a logical extension could have been application for a Ph. D. program, which might point me toward a teaching career. But rather than doing that, I went into the world of work.

I say, "could have been," since later in professional life I learned that I enjoyed teaching more than administrating. But, of course, I didn't know that at the time. While my "niche" could have been in the business field, it also could have been in academe. Which causes me to reflect on the path I followed when I lost my job with Aerospace Composites way back in 1978.

At that time I was married with a family of four. Rather than taking my time to pinpoint the right opportunity, I took the first thing that came along, working as an analyst for a school district. And that particular district was fraught with politics. Although I actually benefited from that environment with two promotions over the four years I worked in the District.

Now that didn't necessarily mean I had found my niche, particularly if it were defined as "administrating." While I failed to note it at the time, the part of that job that I performed best in was the "teaching" part. And my "class" was the Board of Trustees. I excelled at presentations to that Board; everyone told me that, which was nice. But it didn't really dawn on me that I should be in the teaching field. Only with hindsight does it tell me that.

Again, not seeing the forest for the trees. And, again, it happened over and over after that, whether in an elementary school district or in a community college, it was the teaching component that I excelled in. With presentations to Board or to other administrators, it was always the same. I was a "teacher," not an administrator.

Now I had enough clues along the way. When I taught, whether I was a guest lecturer at UC Berkeley, serving as a part-time instructor for Golden Gate University at Castle Air Force Base, or as an adjunct professor at USC, I enjoyed the experience. This was my niche. But, unfortunately, I didn't take the hint. I kept on administrating job after job, even after I received my doctoral degree in public administration.

Only because of a clause in my contract, did I land in a field I seemed to be destined for, full-time teaching in a community college. Regrettably, it took me almost thirty years to figure that all out.

So, whether it's through trial and error or through a more direct approach, the word to the wise is to look for those "niches" throughout your life. And then, and only then, will you realize what you're destined for.

Thanks for listening to my story.

THE END

Exhibits

Exhibit I:
Descendants of Michael Blake

Generation No. 1

Michael Blake was born in Bongard, Germany. He married Maria Christina Ternes on February 26, 1767, in Kradenback, Germany. She was born in Kradenback, Germany, and died on November 5, 1800, in Kradenback, Germany.

Children of Michael Blake and Maria are:

a. Nicholas Blake (No information available)
b. John Joseph Blake, born April 1, 1772, died between 1850 and 1860, St. John the Baptist Church, Johnsburg, Illinois.

Generation No. 2

John Joseph Blake was born on April 1, 1772, in Kradenback, Germany, and died between 1850 and 1860 (St. John the Baptist Church, Johnsburg, Illinois). He married Anna Gertrude Roden. He subsequently married Marie Catherine Schroeder on August 20, 1808, in City Hall Steinenberg, Germany. She was born September 20, 1781, in Mehren, Germany, and died between 1850 and 1860, (St. John the Baptist Church, Johnsburg, Illinois).

Children of John Blake and Anna Roden are:

a. Gertrude Blake, born April 18, 1804.
b. Ann Gertrude Blake, born January 21, 1807.

Children of John Blake and Marie Schroeder are:

a. Jacob Blake, born July 6, 1802.
b. John Adam Blake, born August 25, 1811, Steinenberg, Germany. Died August 9, 1891, Stacyville, Mitchell, Iowa.
c. Maria Elizabeth Blake, born November 23, 1814.
d. Mathias Blake, born June 21, 1816, Steinenberg, Germany, died April 30,1883, (St. Mary's Cemetery, McHenry, Illinois).
e. Philip Blake, born September 22, 1819, Steinenberg, Germany.
f. John Peter Blake, born July 16, 1823, died February 16, 1900, (St. Mary's Cemetery, McHenry, Illinois).

Generation No. 3

Mathias Blake was born on June 21, 1816, in Steinenberg, Germany and died on April 30, 1883 (St. Mary's Cemetery, McHenry, Illinois) He married Margaretha Friesinger on October 30, 1883, in St. Peter and Paul Catholic Church, Demerath, Germany. She was born on February 1, 1813, in Steinenberg, Germany, and died on August 21, 1882, (St. Mary's Catholic Church, McHenry, Illinois).

Children of Mathias Blake and Margaretha Friesinger are:

a. Philip Blake, born September 8, 1841, Steinenberg, Germany, died October 11, 1925, (St. Michael's Catholic Cemetery, Little Falls, Minnesota).
b. Hiram Blake, born 1843.
c. Peter W. Blake, born January 18, 1846, Johnsburg, Illinois, died September 10, 1929, Little Falls, Minnesota.
d. Joseph Blake, born February 18, 1850, Johnsburg, Illinois, died May 7, 1929, Minneapolis, Minnesota.
e. Elizabeth Blake, born August 8, 1851, married John Weingarten. No death date available for Elizabeth.
f. John M. Blake, born February 15, 1853, Johnsburg, McHenry, Illinois, died March 6, 1929, McHenry, Illinois.

Generation No. 4

Peter W. Blake was born on January 18, 1846, in Johnsburg, Illinois, and died on September 10. 1929, in Little Falls, Minnesota. He married Christine Miller on January 24, 1867, in Johnsburg, Illinois, daughter of Jacob Miller and Mary Rothermel. She was born on August 27, 1850, in Johnsburg, Illinois, died November 3, 1936, in Little Falls, Minnesota.

Children of Peter Blake and Christine Miller are:

a. Jacob Blake, born March 28, 1868, Johnsburg, Illinois, died February 8, 1928, St. Paul, Ramsey, Minnesota.
b. Mathias Bartholomew Blake, born October 1, 1869, Johnsburg, Illinois, died January 3, 1928, Little Falls, Minnesota.
c. Joseph B. Blake, born October 2, 1871.
d. Elizabeth Blake, born September 7, 1873.
e. Kathryn Blake, born August 21, 1875.
f. Margaret Blake, Born December 29, 1877.
g. Elizabeth Blake, born May 24, 1880.
h. Mayme Blake, born May 15, 1884.
i. Adeline Blake, born November 5, 1888.

Generation No. 5

Jacob Blake was born on March 28, 1868, in Johnsburg, Illinois, and died on February 8, 1928, St. Paul, Ramsey, Minnesota. He married Adelaide Stump, she died in July 1950, in California.

Children of Jacob Blake and Adelaide Stump are:

a. William Blake, born 1894, died 1963.
b. Christina Blake, born 1895, died 193, married to Herman Von Der Haar.
c. Kathryn Cecelia Blake, born 1896, died 1950, married to Pierce E. Porter.
d. John Henry Blake, born 1898, died 1977, married to Eva Ring.

e. Mary Agnes Blake, born 1900, died 1950, not married.
f. Marcelline Blake, born 1903, died 1905.
g. Margaret Blake, born 1905, died 1975, married to (unnamed).
h. Marcella Blake, born 1909, died 1981.
i. Edward Anthony Blake, born 1909, married Marie Benson, 1938.
j. Reinhart J. Blake, born April 6, 1911, died 1976, married to Grace Ann Reid.
k. Urban Blake, born 1912. Death date unknown.

Generation No. 6

Reinhart J. Blake was born on April 6, 1911, and died on July 13, 1976, (St. Joseph's Cemetery, San Pablo, California). He married Grace Ann Reid in Reno, Nevada, on May 28, 1939. She died on April 9, 1994, (St. Joseph's Cemetery, San Pablo, California).

Children of Reinhart J. Blake and Grace Ann Reid are:

a. Reid U. Blake, born July 12, 1941, in San Rafael, California. He died on January 30, 2016, (St. Joseph's Cemetery, San Pablo, California). He married Gina Bornia on August 4, 1963.
b. Craig T. Blake, born November 2, 1946, in Ross, California. He married Maria Elena Blake, on November 28, 1974.

Generation No. 7

Craig T. Blake was married to Maria Elena Rosales on December 28, 1974. She was born on November 28, 1939.

Children of Craig T. Blake and Maria Elena Rosales are:

a. Matthew J. Blake, born March 24, 1976.
b. Jeffrey R. Blake, born on June 27, 1977.

Craig T. Blake is partner to Rhonda L. Budnick. She was born on January 14,1959.

Generation No. 8

Matthew J. Blake was born on March 24, 1976, and married Jamie Blake on June 7, 2003.

Children of Matthew J. Blake and Jamie Blake are:

a. Jakob Blake, born on May 31, 2005.
b. Noah Blake, born on June 24, 2007.
c. Griffin Blake, born on January 13, 2013.

Jeffrey R. Blake was born on June 27, 1977, and married Loree Carter on August 9, 2008.

Children of Jeffrey R. Blake and Loree Carter are:

a. Eli Blake, born on January 11, 2011.
b. Camdyn Blake, born on October 22, 2012.

Exhibit II:
Record of Education
for Craig Thomas Blake

Grades 1 - 8 St. Anselm's School San Anselmo, CA	1952 - 1960
Grades 9 – 12 Marin Catholic High School Kentfield, CA	1960 - 1964
College of Marin Ross, CA	Summers of 1963, 1964, 1965
University of San Francisco San Francisco, CA	1964 - 1966
UC Berkeley Berkeley, CA B.S. Degree	1966- 1968
UC Berkeley Berkeley, CA M.B.A. Degree	1969 - 1970
University of Southern California Sacramento Public Affairs Center Sacramento, CA D.P.A. Degree	1982 - 1986

Exhibit III:
Professional Employment Record for Craig Thomas Blake

Associate A. T. Kearney & Co. Inc San Francisco, CA	1971
Senior Administrative Analyst University of California, Systemwide Office Berkeley, CA	1972 – 1977
Contract Administrator Aerojet Composites, Inc. San Rafael, CA	1977 - 1978
Principal Budget Analyst Chief, Budgetary Planning Interim Business Manager Oakland Unified School District Oakland, CA	1978 - 1982
Business Manager Orinda Union School District Orinda, CA	1982- 1987
Vice President, Administrative Services Merced Community College District Merced, CA	1987 -1992
Associate Chancellor San Mateo CCCD San Mateo, CA	1992-1999

Exhibit IV: Academic Employment Record for Craig Thomas Blake

Guest Lecturer Public Sector Budgeting UC Berkeley Berkeley, CA	Fall 1978
Adjunct Professor Quantitative Methods University of Southern California Sacramento, CA	Spring 1982
Instructor Public Finance Golden Gate University Castle Air Force Base Atwater, CA	Fall 1988
Professor Business & Management College of San Mateo San Mateo, CA	Fall 2000 – Spring 2010

Exhibit V:
Record of Residences Owned
by Craig Thomas Blake*

2684 Shady Draw Pinole, CA Current Value: $859,300	1975 - 1976
2624 Simas Avenue Pinole, CA Current Value: $963,800	1977 – 1987
1585 Santa Inez Court Merced, CA Current Value: $504,500	1987 – 1992
305 Eagle Trace Half Moon Bay, CA Current Value: $2,016,600	1992 – 1999
132 Patrick Way Half Moon Bay, CA Current Value: $1,149,000	2000 - 2014
16300 Texas Springs Road Redding, CA Current Value: $912,400	2013 - Present

* Current Value as of September 14, 2021

Exhibit VI: Record of Vehicles Owned by Craig Thomas Blake

1. Used 1956 Pontiac Catalina, Coupe, Blue, Automatic, acquired 1962.
2. Used 1962 Pontiac Catalina, Coupe, Blue, Automatic, acquired 1964.
3. Used 1969 Chevrolet Camaro, Coupe, Blue, Automatic, acquired 1971.
4. New 1973 Datsun 240Z, Coupe, Silver, Manual, acquired 1973.
5. New 1979 Mazda RX-7, Coupe, Metallic Blue, Manual, acquired 1979.
6. Used 1986 Porsche 944 Turbo, Coupe, Torch Red, Manual, acquired 1986.
7. New 1992 Mazda Miata, Convertible, Black, Manual, acquired 1992.
8. New 1996 Porsche Cabriolet, Torch Red, Manual, acquired 1996.
9. New 1999 Mazda Miata, Convertible, Forest Green, Manual, acquired 1999.
10. New 2002 Audi TT Roadster, Convertible, Silver, Manual, acquired 2002.
11. New 2005 Porsche 911 Cabriolet, Silver, Manual, acquired 2005.
12. New 2006 Porsche 911S Cabriolet, Black, Manual, acquired 2006.
13. New 2010 Chevrolet Camaro, Coupe, Red, Manual, acquired 2010.
14. New 2012 Chevrolet Corvette, Coupe, Blue, Manual, acquired 2012.
15. New 2014 Jaguar F-Type, Convertible, Black, Automatic, acquired 2014.
16. Used 2012 Porsche 911 S Cabriolet, Red, Manual, acquired 2016.
17. New 2019 Chevrolet Corvette Z06, Convertible, Manual, acquired 2019.

Exhibit VII a: Cast of Characters, Relatives

Name *	Relationship **
1. Adelaide Blake	Grandmother
2. Albert Reid	Grandfather
3. Aunt Alice	Mother's sister
4. Aunt Chris	Father's sister
5. Aunt Helen	Mother's sister
6. Aunt Marce	Father's sister
7. Aunt Marian	Father's sister-in-law
8. Aunt Marie	Aunt in Minnesota
9. Bill Foerstler	Cousin's husband
10. Bub	Aunt Helen's husband
11. Camdyn Blake	Granddaughter
12. Carol	Herman's wife
13. Cece	Cousin
14. Cesarino	Gina's brother
15. Claire Foerstler	Cousin
16. David Blake	Cousin
17. Ellen Blake	Relative
18. Elena	Spouse
19. Eli Blake	Grandson
20. Elizabeth	Cousin
21. Gina Blake	Sister-in-law
22. Grace Blake	Mother
23. Griffin Blake	Grandson
24. Herman	Cousin
25. Jack	Lucille's second husband
26. Jocko	Lucille's first husband
27. Jack Pierce	Uncle by marriage
28. Jacob Blake	Grandfather
29. Jakob Blake	Grandson

30. Jamie Blake	Daughter-in-law
31. Jeffrey Blake	Son
32. Julie Epling	Gina's cousin
33. Junior	Cousin
34. Kathryn Blake Porter	Pierce's wife
35. Ken Blake	Ellen Blake's husband
36. Ken DeLaca	Cece's husband
37. Loree Blake	Daughter-in-law
38. Lucille	Cousin
39. Matthew Blake	Son
40. Uncle Billy	Aunt Chris's son
41. Uncle Herman	Godfather
42. Nephew/cousin	Nephew/cousin
43. Noah Blake	Grandson
44. Pam	Cousin
45. Pauline	Cousin Billy's wife
46. Pierce Porter	Aunt's husband
47. Reid Blake	Brother
48. Reinhart Blake	Father
49. Rhonda	Partner
50. Roger Blake	Cousin
51. Scott Blake	Nephew/godson
52. Steven Blake	Nephew
53. Stephen Foerstler	Cousin
54. Vickie Von der Haar	Cousin

Exhibit VII b: Cast of Characters, Friends

Name	Relationship
1. Amanda (pseudonym)	Girlfriend
2. Christine	Girlfriend
3. Danny	High school friend
4. Darwin	Co-worker friend
5. Dee	Co-worker friend
6. Eleanor (pseudonym)	Co-worker friend
7. Leo	Co-worker friend
8. Guati	Best friend
9. Jeff	Loree's father
10. Jim	School friend
11. Joey DePatta	School friend
12. Julie Epling	Friend
13. Kevin	Sailing friend
14. Michael	Neighbor friend
15. Mike	Friend
16. Mohan	UC co-worker
17. Peter	School friend
18. Phil	School friend
19. Ron (pseudonym)	School friend
20. Roger	Roommate friend
21. Sally	Girlfriend
22. Ted (pseudonym)	Best friend
23. Todd	Neighbor friend
24. Vicky	Summer girlfriend
25. Vicky	Neighbor friend

Exhibit VII c: Cast of Characters, Employers

	Name	Relationship
1.	Charles Mitchell	OUSD administrator
2.	Darwin	SMCCCD administrator
3.	David Bowick	OUSD superintendent
4.	Dee	SMCCD secretary
5.	Eleanor (pseudonym)	Orinda secretary
6.	Elena	UC employee
7.	Frances	MCCD manager
8.	Jim	Insurance intern
9.	Lana	UC secretary
10.	Laura (pseudonym)	SMCCCD manager
11.	Leo	Insurance intern
12.	Lolly	SMCCCD worker
13.	Mark	Insurance intern
14.	Marvin	MCCD manager
15.	Mohan	UC employee
16.	Patricia (pseudonym)	Insurance secretary
17.	Ralph (pseudonym)	Wells Fargo supervisor
18.	Rhonda	SMCCCD manager
19.	Ruth Love	OUSD superintendent
20.	Susan	MCCD librarian

Exhibit VII d: Cast of Characters, Classmates

Name	Relationship
1. Amanda (pseudonym)	High school
2. Ang-Kiat Poo	MBA program
3. Big Guy	High school
4. Buzz	Grammar school
5. Danny	High school
6. Frankie	Grammar school
7. Jim	High school/USF
8. Jim	UC student
9. Joey De Patta	High school
10. John	Lottery director
11. Julie Epling	High school
12. Kevin	High school
13. Leo	UC student
14. Mark	UC student
15. Michael	Grammar school
16. Mike Epling	MBA program
17. Peter	High school/UC
18. Phil	High school/USF
19. Richard Stevens	Grammar school
20. Rod	Lab partner
21. Roger	USF roommate
22. Ron (pseudonym)	High school/USF
23. Sandra (pseudonym)	High school
24. Sheila (pseudonym)	USC doctoral program
25. Ted (pseudonym)	High school/UC
26. Tall Guy	High school

Exhibit VII e: Cast of Characters, Teachers & Advisors

	Name	Relationship
1.	Father Dullea	MCHS principal
2.	Gary Hoaglander	USC advisor
3.	Jeffrey Chapman	USC advisor
4.	Jim	MCHS teacher
5.	John Kirlin	USC advisor
6.	Leonard Merewitz	MBA advisor
7.	Mrs. Marks	Teacher/4th grade
8.	Sister Eulalie Rose	Teacher/2nd grade
9.	Sister Benigna	Teacher /8th grade

Exhibit VII f: Cast of Other Characters

	Name	Relationship
1.	Barry the Swede	Reid's friend
2.	Chip	Pontiac salesman
3.	Father Benz	Altar boy founder
4.	Inventory Frank	Purity Stores mgr.
5.	Mable	Purity Store clerk
6.	Mar McGregor	Plastic surgeon
7.	Mr. Servante	Civil engineer
8.	Mrs. Loggie	Landlord
9.	Mrs. Otten	Blake theorist
10.	Mrs. Sabatini (pseudonym)	Morningside neighbor
11.	Russian Bride	Ted's fiancé
12.	Sadowski brothers	Morningside neighbors
13.	Sam Something	Bus driver
14.	Stoddard	DMV examiner
15.	Ted's uncle priest	St. Vincent's priest

*As used in memoir
**Relationship to Craig Thomas Blake

Index

C

D

E

F

G

H

I

J

K

L

M

N

O

P

Q

R

S

T

U

V

W

X

Y

Z

Amazon Reader Reviews of Author's Novels:

In Search of Sarah: A Time Traveler's Quandary

"A hard book to put down, page after page kept me guessing."

"Keep-your-mind-thinking kind of book. Cannot wait for the sequel!"

Dark Matters: In Search of Mackenzie

"With an interesting premise established at the outset, the story draws the reader into fascinating worlds."

"A completely satisfying read ... You'll find yourself rooting for Mackenzie and Jeff as they wind their paths forward ..."

Dark Futures

"Another edge-of-your-seat adventure filled with formidable obstacles and surprising turns."

"The story keeps you guessing all the way to the exciting conclusion. Definitely a must read!"

CPSIA information can be obtained
at www.ICGtesting.com
Printed in the USA
BVHW081240020222
627783BV00001B/99

9 781636 830223